THE
CROWN OF SORROW
LENT

*MEDITATIONS ON THE PASSION OF
OUR LORD*

FIRST AMERICAN EDITION

BY THE
MOST REV. ALBAN GOODIER, S.J.
AUTHOR OF "THE PRINCE OF PEACE," "THE MEANING
OF LIFE," ETC.

A GRAIL

ST. MEINRAD

Nihil Obstat.

    FRANCISCUS M. CANONICUS WYNDHAM,
      Censor Deputatus.

Imprimatur.

    EDM. CAN. SURMONT,
      Vicarius Generalis.

Westmonasterii,
    Die 16 Maii, 1918.

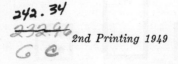

    2nd Printing 1949

BY SPECIAL ARRANGEMENT WITH
BURNS OATES & WASHBOURNE LTD.
PUBLISHERS TO THE HOLY SEE
LONDON

CONTENTS

CONTENTS

THE CROWN OF SORROW

THE PASSION OF OUR LORD JESUS CHRIST IN THE WORDS OF THE FOUR EVANGELISTS

1. AND when Jesus had said these things, and they had sung a hymn, He went forth with His disciples, according to the custom, over the brook Cedron to the Mount of Olives, where there was a garden. Then Jesus saith to them: You will all be scandalized in Me this night. For it is written: I will strike the shepherd, and the sheep of the flock shall be dispersed. But after I shall be risen again, I will go before you into Galilee.

2. But Peter answering said to Him: Although all men shall be scandalized in Thee, I will never be scandalized. And Jesus saith to him: Amen I say to thee, to-day, even this night, before the cock crow twice, thou shalt deny Me thrice. But Peter spoke the more vehemently and saith to Him: Although I should die together with Thee, I will not deny Thee. And in like manner also said they all.

3. Then Jesus came with them to a country place, a farm, which is called Gethsemani. And He said to His disciples: Sit you here, till I go yonder and pray. Pray, lest ye enter into temp-

tation. And taking with Him Peter, and James and John the two sons of Zebedee, He began to grow sorrowful and to be sad, to fear and to be heavy. Then He saith to them: My soul is sorrowful even unto death, stay you here and watch with Me.

4. And when He had gone forward a little, and was withdrawn away from them a stone's cast, kneeling down He fell flat on the ground upon His face: and He prayed, saying: Father, if Thou wilt, remove this chalice from Me, Nevertheless not as I will, but as Thou wilt. Abba, Father, all things are possible to Thee. Take away this chalice from Me. But not what I will, but what Thou wilt.

5. And He cometh to His disciples and findeth them asleep. And He saith to Peter: Simon, sleepest thou? What! Couldst thou, could you, not watch one hour with Me? Watch ye: and pray that ye enter not into temptation. The spirit indeed is willing, but the flesh is weak.

6. And going away again He went the second time, and prayed, saying the selfsame words: O My Father, if this chalice cannot pass except I drink it, Thy will be done. And He cometh again and findeth them asleep, for their eyes were heavy with sorrow. And He said to them: Why sleep you? Arise, pray, lest you enter into temptation. And they knew not what to answer Him.

7. And leaving them He went away again, and He prayed the third time, saying the same words. And there appeared to Him an Angel from Heaven, strengthening Him. And being in an agony He prayed the longer. And His sweat became as drops of blood trickling down upon the ground. Then He cometh the third time to His disciples and saith to them: Sleep ye on now and take your rest. It is enough; the hour is come. Behold the hour is at hand, and the Son of Man shall be betrayed into the hands of sinners. Rise up: let us go. Behold he that will betray Me is at hand.

8. Now Judas also, who betrayed Him, one of the twelve, knew the place, because Jesus had often resorted thither together with His disciples. Judas, therefore, having received a band of men and servants from the chief priests and the Pharisees, the scribes and the ancients of the people, cometh thither while He was yet speaking, and with him a great multitude, with lanterns and torches and weapons, swords and clubs and staves.

9. Jesus, therefore, knowing all things that were to come upon Him, went forward and saith to them: Whom seek ye? They answered Him: Jesus of Nazareth. Jesus saith to them: I am He. And Judas also, who betrayed Him, stood with them. As soon, then, as He had said to them, I am He, they went backward and fell to the ground. Again, therefore, He asked them:

3

Whom seek ye? And they said: Jesus of Nazareth. Jesus answered: I have told you that I am He. If therefore you seek Me, let these go their way; that the word might be fulfilled which He said: Of them whom Thou hast given Me, I have not lost anyone.

10. And he that betrayed Him had given them a sign, saying: Whomsoever I shall kiss, that is He; lay hold on Him, hold Him fast, and lead Him away cautiously. And when he was come, immediately going up to Jesus, he said: Hail, Rabbi, and he kissed Him. And Jesus said to him: Friend, whereto art thou come? Judas, dost thou betray the Son of Man with a kiss? Then they came up, and laid hands on Jesus, and held Him.

11. And they that were about Him, seeing what would follow, said to Him: Lord, shall we strike with the sword? Then one of them that was with Jesus, Simon Peter, stretching forth his hand, drew his sword, and striking the servant of the high priest, cut off his ear. And the name of the servant was Malchus. But Jesus, answering, said: Suffer ye thus far. Then He said to Peter: Put up again thy sword into the scabbard. For all that take the sword shall perish with the sword. Thinkest thou that I cannot ask My Father, and He will give Me presently more than twelve legions of angels? How, then, shall the Scriptures be fulfilled, that so it must be done? The chalice which My

4

Father hath given me, shall I not drink it? And when He had touched his ear, He healed him.

12. In that same hour Jesus said to the chief priests and magistrates of the Temple, and the ancients and the multitude that were come to Him: Are you come out, as it were against a robber, with swords and clubs and staves to apprehend Me? I sat daily with you teaching in the Temple, and you did not stretch forth your hand against Me. But this is your hour, and the power of darkness. Now all this was done, that the Scriptures of the prophets might be fulfilled. Then His disciples, leaving Him, all fled away. And a certain young man followed Him, having a linen cloth cast about his naked body, and they laid hold on him. But he, casting off the linen cloth, fled from them naked.

13. Then the band, and the tribune, and the servants of the Jews, took Jesus and bound Him. And they led Him away to Annas first, for he was father-in-law to Caiphas, who was the high priest of that year. Now Caiphas was he who had given the counsel to the Jews, that it was expedient that one man should die for the people.

14. The high priest then asked Jesus of His disciples and His doctrine. Jesus answered him: I have spoken openly to the world, I have always taught in the synagogue and in the Temple whither all the Jews resort, and in private I

have spoken nothing. Why askest thou Me? Ask
them who have heard what I have spoken to
them; behold, they know what things I have
said. And when He had said these things, one
of the officers standing by gave Jesus a blow,
saying: Answerest Thou the high priest so?
Jesus answered him: If I have spoken ill, give
testimony of the evil; but if well, why strikest
thou Me? And Annas sent Him bound to
Caiphas, the high priest.

15. But they, holding Jesus, led Him to Caiphas, the high priest, and all the priests and the
scribes and the ancients were assembled together. And the chief priests and the whole council
sought false witness for evidence against Jesus,
that they might put Him to death. For though
many false witnesses had come in, and bore
false witness against Him, their evidence did
not agree. And last of all there came in two
false witnesses. They, rising up, bore false
witness against Him, saying: We heard Him
say, I will destroy this temple of God made with
hands, and within three days I will build another
not made with hands. And their witness did
not agree.

16. And the high priest, rising up in the
midst, asked Jesus, saying: Answerest Thou
nothing to the things that are laid to Thy charge
by these men? But Jesus held His peace and
answered nothing. Again the high priest asked
Him and said to Him: I adjure Thee, by the

living God, that Thou tell us if Thou be the
Christ, the Son of the blessed God. And Jesus
said to him: Thou hast said it, I am. Nevertheless I say to you, hereafter you shall see
the Son of Man sitting on the right hand of
the power of God, and coming in the clouds of
Heaven. Then the high priest rent his garments,
saying: He hath blasphemed; what further need
have we of witnesses? Behold, now you have
heard the blasphemy, what think you? But they
all answering, condemned Him and said: He is
guilty of death.

17. But Simon Peter followed Jesus afar off,
and so did another disciple, to the high priest's
palace. And that disciple was known to the high
priest, and went in with Jesus into the court
of the high priest. But Peter stood at the door
without. Then the other disciple, who was known
to the high priest, went out and spoke to the
portress, and brought in Peter. And when they
had kindled a fire of coals in the midst of the
hall, because it was cold, and were sitting about
it, Peter sat with the servants to see the end,
and warmed himself. Now when Peter was in
the court below, there cometh one of the maidservants of the high priest, the maid that was
portress; and when she had seen Peter sitting
in the light and warming himself, and had
looked on him, she said: Thou also wast with
Jesus of Nazareth, the Galilean. This man also
was with Him. Art not thou also one of this

7

man's disciples? But he denied Him before them all, saying: Woman, I am not. I know Him not. I neither know nor understand what thou sayest.

18. And he went forth before the court, out of the gate, and the cock crew. And again another maidservant saw him, and she began to say to the standers-by: This is one of them. This man also was with Jesus of Nazareth. Thou also art one of them. And again he denied with an oath: O man, I am not. I do not know the man. And after a little while, about the space of one hour after, they that stood by came and said to Peter: Surely thou also art one of them, for even thy speech doth discover thee. Thou also art a Galilaean. And another man, one of the servants of the high priest, a kinsman to him whose ear Peter cut off, saith to him: Did I not see thee in the Garden with Him? Then he began to curse and swear that he knew not the man, saying: Man, I know not what thou sayest; I know not this man of whom you speak.

19. And immediately, while he was yet speaking, the cock crew again. And the Lord, turning, looked on Peter. And Peter remembered the word that the Lord Jesus had said to him: Before the cock crow twice thou shalt deny Me thrice. And Peter went out, and began to weep, and wept bitterly.

20. And the men that held Him began to spit in His face, and mocked Him, and buffeted

8

Him, and they blindfolded Him, and covered His face, and smote Him in the face, and the servants struck Him with the palms of their hands. And they asked Him, saying: Prophesy unto us, O Christ, who is he that struck Thee? And many other things, blaspheming, they said against Him.

21. And as soon as it was day, straightway all the chief priests and ancients of the people and scribes came together and held a council against Jesus to put Him to death. And they brought Him into their council, saying: If Thou be the Christ, tell us. And He said to them: If I shall tell you, you will not believe Me, and if I shall also ask you, you will not answer me nor let Me go. But hereafter the Son of Man shall be sitting on the right hand of the power of God. Then said they all: Art Thou then the Son of God? And He said: You say that I am. Then said they all: What need we any further testimony? For we ourselves have heard it from His own mouth. And the whole multitude of them rose up, and led Him away bound, and delivered Him to Pontius Pilate the Governor.

22. Then Judas, who betrayed Him, seeing that He was condemned, repenting himself, brought back the thirty pieces of silver to the chief priests and ancients, saying: I have sinned in betraying innocent blood. But they said: What is that to us? look thou to it. And casting

9

down the pieces of silver in the Temple, he departed and went and hanged himself with a halter. But the chief priests, having taken the pieces of silver, said: It is unlawful for us to put them into the corbona, because it is the price of blood. And having consulted together, they bought with them the potter's field, to be a burying-place for strangers. Wherefore that field was called Haceldama, that is, the field of blood, even to this day. Then was fulfilled that which was spoken by Jeremias the Prophet, saying: And they took the thirty pieces of silver, the price of Him that was valued, whom they prized of the children of Israel. And they gave them unto the potter's field, as the Lord appointed to me.

23. Then they led Jesus from Caiphas to the Governor's hall. And it was morning, and they went not into the hall, that they might not be defiled, but that they might eat the Pasch. Pilate therefore went out to meet them, and said: What accusation bring you against this man? They answered and said to him: If He were not a malefactor, we would not have delivered Him up to thee.

24. Pilate then said to them: Take Him you, and judge Him according to your law. The Jews therefore said to him: It is not lawful for us to put anyone to death; that the word of Jesus might be fulfilled, signifying what death He should die. And they began to accuse Him,

saying: We have found this man perverting our nation, and forbidding to give tribute to Caesar, and saying that He is Christ the King. And Jesus stood before Pilate the Governor. And Pilate asked Him, saying: Art Thou the King of the Jews? And Jesus answered him and said: Thou sayest it. And the chief priest and ancients accused Him in many things. And when He was accused He answered nothing.

25. Then Pilate again asked Him: Answerest Thou nothing? Behold in how many things they accuse Thee. Dost not Thou hear how great testimonies they allege against Thee? But Jesus still answered him not to any word, so that the Governor wondered exceedingly. Pilate therefore went into the hall again, and called Jesus, and said to Him: Art Thou the King of the Jews? Jesus answered: Sayest thou this thing of thyself, or have others told it thee of Me? Pilate answered: Am I a Jew? Thy nation and the chief priests have delivered Thee up to me. What hast Thou done? Jesus answered: My Kingdom is not of this world. If My Kingdom were of this world, My servants would certainly strive that I should not be delivered to the Jews, but now My Kingdom is not from hence. Pilate therefore said to Him: Art Thou a King then? Jesus answered: Thou sayest that I am a King. For this was I born, and for this came I into the world, that I should give testimony to the truth. Everyone that is of the truth heareth

11

My voice. Pilate saith to Him: What is truth? And when he had said this he went forth again to the Jews, and saith to them: I find no cause in Him.

26. But they were more earnest, saying: He stirreth up the people, teaching throughout all Judea, beginning from Galilee to this place. And Pilate hearing of Galilee, asked if the man were a Galilean. And when he understood that He belonged to Herod's jurisdiction, he sent Him away to Herod, who himself was also at Jerusalem in those days.

27. And Herod, seeing Jesus, was very glad, for he was desirous of a long time to see Him, because he had heard many things of Him, and he hoped to see some miracle wrought by Him. And he questioned Him with many words. But He answered him nothing. And the chief priests and scribes stood by, earnestly accusing Him. And Herod with his soldiers despised Him, and mocked Him, putting on Him a white garment, and sent Him back to Pilate. And Herod and Pilate were made friends together that same day: for before they were enemies one to another.

28. Then Pilate, calling together the chief priests and the magistrates of the people, said to them: You have brought this man to me as one that perverteth the people; and behold, I, having examined Him before you, find no cause in this man touching those things wherein you

12

accuse Him. No, nor yet Herod, for I sent you to him, and behold, nothing worthy of death is done to Him. I will chastise Him, therefore, and release Him.

29. Now upon the solemn festival-day the Governor was accustomed to release to the people one of the prisoners, whomsoever they demanded. And he had then a notorious prisoner that was called Barabbas, a robber who was put in prison with seditious men, who in the sedition had committed murder. And when the multitude was come up, they began to desire what he always had done to them. And Pilate answered them and said: You have a custom that I should release one unto you at the Pasch. Will you, therefore, that I release unto you the King of the Jews? Whom will you that I release to you, Barabbas, or Jesus who is called Christ? For he knew that through envy the chief priests had delivered Him up.

30. But the chief priests and ancients persuaded the people that they should ask Barabbas and make Jesus away. And the Governor answering said to them: Which will you have of the two to be released unto you? But the whole multitude cried out at once, saying: Away with this man, and release unto us Barabbas. And Pilate spoke to them again, desiring to release Jesus: What will you then that I do with Jesus, that is called Christ, the King of the Jews? But they all again cried out: Crucify Him,

crucify Him, crucify Him, let Him be crucified!
And Pilate said to them the third time: Why,
what evil hath He done? I find no cause of
death in Him. I will chastise Him, therefore,
and let Him go. But they were the more instant
with loud voices: Crucify Him, let Him be
crucified! And their voices prevailed.

31. And Pilate, seeing that he prevailed nothing, but rather that a tumult was made, having
taken water, washed his hands before the people,
saying: I am innocent of the blood of this just
man; look you to it. And all the people answering said: His blood be upon us and upon our
children. Then Pilate, being willing to satisfy
the people, gave sentence that their petition
should be granted. And he released unto them
Barabbas, who for murder and sedition had been
cast into prison, whom they had desired, but
delivered up to them Jesus, when he had
scourged Him, to be crucified according to their
will.

32. Then the soldiers of the Governor, taking
Jesus into the court of the palace, gathered
together unto Him the whole band, and stripping
Him, they put a scarlet cloak about Him. And
platting a crown of thorns, they put it upon
His head, and a reed in His right hand. And
they came to Him, and bowing the knee before
Him, they mocked Him, and began to salute
Him, saying: Hail, King of the Jews! And they
gave Him blows, and they did spit upon Him,

14

and they took the reed and struck His head, and bowing their knees, they worshipped Him.

33. Pilate therefore went forth again and saith to them: Behold I bring Him forth to you, that you may know that I find no cause in Him. (So Jesus came forth, bearing the crown of thorns, and the purple garment.) And he saith to them: Behold the man! When the chief priests, therefore, and the officers had seen Him, they cried out, saying: Crucify Him, crucify Him! Pilate saith to them: Take Him you, and crucify Him, for I find no cause in Him. The Jews answered him: We have a law, and according to that law He ought to die, because He made Himself the Son of God.

34. When Pilate therefore had heard this saying he feared the more. And he entered into the hall again, and he said to Jesus: Whence art Thou? But Jesus gave him no answer. Pilate therefore saith to Him: Speakest Thou not to me? Knowest Thou not that I have power to crucify Thee, and I have power to release Thee? Jesus answered: Thou shouldst not have any power against Me, unless it were given thee from above. Therefore he that hath delivered Me to thee hath the greater sin.

35. And from thenceforth Pilate sought to release Him. But the Jews cried out, saying: If thou release this man thou art not Caesar's friend, for whosoever maketh himself a king speaketh against Caesar. Now when Pilate had

heard these words, he brought Jesus forth, and
sat down in the judgment-seat, in the place that
is called Lithostrotos, and in Hebrew Gabbatha.
And it was the Parasceve of the Pasch, about
the sixth hour, and he saith to the Jews: Behold your King! But they cried out: Away with
Him, away with Him, crucify Him! Pilate saith
to them: Shall I crucify your King? The chief
priests answered: We have no king but Caesar.
Then therefore, he delivered Him to them to
be crucified.

36. And after they had mocked Him, they
took off the purple cloak from Him, and put on
Him His own garments, and led Him away to
crucify Him. And as they led Him away, they
found a man of Cyrene, named Simon, who
passed by coming out of the country, the father
of Alexander and of Rufus; him they forced to
take up His cross to carry after Jesus.

37. And there followed Him a great multitude
of people and of women, who bewailed and lamented Him. But Jesus, turning to them, said:
Daughters of Jerusalem, weep not over Me, but
weep for yourselves and for your children. For,
behold, the day shall come wherein they will
say: Blessed are the barren and the wombs
that have not borne, and the breasts that have
not given suck. Then shall they begin to say
to the mountains: Fall upon us, and to the hills:
Cover us. For if in the green wood they do
these things, what shall be done in the dry?

38. And bearing His own cross, He went forth to that place which is called Calvary, but in Hebrew Golgotha. And they gave Him to drink wine mingled with myrrh. And when He had tasted He would not drink. And there were also two others, malefactors, led with Him to be put to death. And when they were come to the place they crucified Him there; and the robbers, one on the right hand, and the other on the left. And the Scripture was fulfilled, which saith: And with the wicked He was reputed.

39. And Pilate wrote a title also, and he put it upon the cross over His head. And the writing was: This is Jesus of Nazareth, the King of the Jews. This title, therefore, many of the Jews read, because the place where Jesus was crucified was near to the city, and it was written in Hebrew, in Greek, and in Latin. Then the chief priests said to Pilate: Write not, the King of the Jews, but that He said: I am the King of the Jews. Pilate answered: What I have written I have written.

40. And Jesus said: Father, forgive them, for they know not what they do. Then the soldiers, after they had crucified Him, took his garments (and they made four parts, to every soldier a part, casting lots upon them what every man should take), and also His coat. Now the coat was without seam, woven from the top throughout. They said to one another: Let us not cut it, but let us cast lots for it whose it shall

be; that the word might be fulfilled which was spoken by the Prophet: They have parted My garments among them, and upon My vesture they have cast lots. And the soldiers indeed did these things. And it was the third hour and they crucified Him.

41. And they sat down and watched Him. And the people stood beholding. And they that passed by blasphemed Him, wagging their heads and saying: Vah, Thou that destroyest the Temple of God, and in three days buildest it up again, save Thy own self: if Thou be the Son of God, come down from the cross. In like manner the chief priests with the scribes and ancients, mocking, derided Him, saying: He saved others, Himself He cannot save. If He be Christ the King of Israel, if He be Christ the Son of God, let Him now come down from the cross, that we may see and believe. He trusted in God; let Him now deliver Him, if He will have Him, for He said: I am the Son of God.

42. And the soldiers also mocked Him, coming to Him and offering Him vinegar, and saying: If Thou be the King of the Jews, save Thyself. And the selfsame thing the thieves that were crucified with Him reproached Him with, and reviled Him. And one of these robbers who were hanging, blasphemed Him, saying: If thou be Christ, save Thyself and us. But the other, answering, rebuked him, saying: Neither dost

thou fear God, seeing thou art under the same condemnation? And we, indeed, justly, for we receive the due reward of our deeds; but this man hath done no evil. And he said to Jesus: Lord, remember me when Thou shalt come into Thy kingdom. And Jesus said to him: Amen, I say to thee, this day thou shalt be with Me in Paradise.

43. Now there stood by the cross of Jesus His Mother, and His Mother's sister, Mary of Cleophas, and Mary Magdalen. When Jesus therefore saw His Mother, and the disciple standing whom He loved, He saith to His Mother: Woman, behold thy son. After that He saith to the disciple: Behold thy Mother. And from that hour the disciple took her to his own.

44. And when the sixth hour was come, there was darkness over the whole earth until the ninth hour. And about the ninth hour Jesus cried out with a loud voice, saying: Eloi, Eloi, lamma sabacthani? which is, being interpreted: My God, My God, why hast Thou forsaken Me? And some of them that stood there and heard, said: Behold, this man calleth for Elias.

45. Afterwards Jesus, knowing that all things were accomplished, that the Scripture might be fulfilled, said: I thirst. Now there was a vessel set there full of vinegar. And immediately one of them running took a sponge and filled it with vinegar and put it on a reed about hyssop, and offered it to His mouth, and gave Him to drink.

And others said: Stay, let us see whether Elias will come to take Him down and deliver Him. When Jesus therefore had taken the vinegar, He said: It is consummated.

46. And Jesus again crying with a loud voice, said: Father, into Thy hands I commend My Spirit. And saying this, bowing down His head, He gave up the ghost. And behold the sun was darkened, and the veil of the Temple was rent in two in the midst from the top even to the bottom, and the earth quaked, and the rocks were rent. And the graves opened, and many bodies of the Saints that had slept arose, and coming out of the tombs after His resurrection, came into the holy city and appeared to many.

47. Now the centurion, who stood over against Him, and they that were with him watching Jesus, seeing that crying out in this manner He had given up the ghost; having seen the earthquake and the things that were done, were greatly afraid, and glorified God, saying: Indeed this was a just man. Indeed this man was the Son of God.

48. And all the multitude of them that were come together to that sight, and saw the things that were done, returned striking their breasts. And there were also women, among whom was Mary Magdalene, and Mary the mother of James the Less, and of Joseph, and Salome, and the mother of the sons of Zebedee, who also when He was in Galilee followed Him, and ministered

to Him, and many other women that came up with Him to Jerusalem. And all His acquaintance and the women stood afar off beholding these things.

49. Then the Jews (because it was the Parasceve), that the bodies might not remain upon the cross on the Sabbath day (for that was a great Sabbath day), besought Pilate that their legs might be broken, and that they might be taken away. The soldiers therefore came, and they broke the legs of the first, and of the other that was crucified with Him. But when they came to Jesus, and saw that He was already dead, they did not break His legs, but one of the soldiers opened His side with a spear, and immediately there came out blood and water. And he that saw gave testimony, and his testimony is true. And he knoweth that he saith true, that you also may believe. For these things were done that the Scripture might be fulfilled: You shall not break a bone of Him. And again another Scripture saith: They shall look on Him whom they pierced.

50. And when evening was come (because it was the Parasceve, that is, the day before the Sabbath), a certain rich man of Arimathea, a city of Judea, by name Joseph, who was a senator, a noble councillor, a good and just man, who also himself waited for the Kingdom of God, and was a disciple of Jesus, but in private for fear of the Jews; this man had not con-

sented to their counsel and doings; went in boldly to Pilate and besought that he might take away the body of Jesus. But Pilate wondered that He should be already dead. And when he had understood it by the centurion, he commanded that the body of Jesus should be delivered to Joseph. He came therefore and took away the body of Jesus.

51. And Nicodemus also came, who at first came to Jesus by night, bringing a mixture of myrrh and aloes, about a hundred pounds. They took therefore the body of Jesus, and buying fine linen, wrapped it up in the linen cloths with the spices, as it is the custom with the Jews to bury. And there was in the place where He was crucified a garden, and in the garden a new sepulchre, his own (Joseph's) monument, which he had hewed out in a rock, wherein never yet any man had been laid. There, therefore, by reason of the Parasceve of the Jews, they laid Jesus, because the sepulchre was nigh at hand. And he rolled a great stone to the door of the monument, and went his way. And Mary Magdalen, and Mary the mother of Joseph, and, the women that were come with Him from Galilee, following after, sitting over against the sepulchre, beheld where His body was laid. And returning they prepared spices and ointments, and on the Sabbath day they rested, according to the commandment.

52. And the next day which followed the day

of the preparation, the chief priests and the Pharisees came together to Pilate, saying: Sir, we have remembered that that seducer said, while He was yet alive: After three days I will rise again. Command, therefore, the sepulchre to be guarded until the third day, lest His disciples come, and steal Him away, and say to the people: He is risen from the dead, so the last error shall be worse than the first. Pilate said to them: You have a guard; go, guard it as you know. And they, departing, made the sepulchre sure with guards, sealing the stone.

I.—THE LEAVE-TAKING

*"And when Jesus had said these things, and they
had sung a hymn, He went forth with His disciples,
according to His custom, over the brook Cedron to
the Mount of Olives, where there was a garden.
Then Jesus saith to them, You will all be scandalized
in Me this night. For it is written: I will strike the
shepherd, and the sheep of the flock shall be dispersed. But after I shall be risen again, I will go
before you into Galilee."—Matt. xxvi. 30-32; Mark
xiv. 26-28; Luke xxii. 39; John xviii. 1.*

1. Our Lord knew that this was to be the last
gathering. At the beginning of the Last Supper
He had said: "With desire I have desired (*i.e.*,
I have desired with great longing) to eat this
Pasch with you before I suffer." All through
that Supper how keen was His affection for
His own; how much He felt for them; how all
His words and actions had been directed with
a view to giving them comfort and courage!
He had bid farewell to His Mother; of that
scene, as of all other similar scenes, Scripture
tells us not a word, as though the Evangelists
felt it to be too sacred for description. But it
is not too sacred for meditation, and we may
look on, and say and think what we will. He
bade farewell to Judas in unmistakable terms;
but with how much affection it had been pre-
ceded, how much affection was shown even at
the parting itself! And He bade farewell to
all the rest; we can take them one by one, with

their different characters and different short-
comings, and know that He had a special love
for each.

2. Then He led them out for the last walk
together in the evening twilight. They were full
of courage, for had they not been fed with His
own Body and His own Blood? Full of hope,
for had He not told them that He had overcome
the world? Full of thankfulness, for had He not
prayed specially for them and associated them
with Himself before His Father. "Heavenly
Father," He had said, "I pray that where I
am, these may also be." But, lastly, full of
confidence in themselves; they had not yet
learned that "Without Me you can do nothing."
This Our Lord knew, though they did not; and
it is the one piercing agony of the leave-taking.
He must tell them. In spite of all their joy
of heart, and protestations, He says to them:
"You will all be scandalized in Me this night:
For it is written, I will strike the Shepherd, and
the sheep of the flock shall be dispersed."

3. There is something very tender in the
manner of this solemn warning. He scarcely
seems to blame them; He speaks as if it were a
sad necessity, and quotes a prophecy to confirm
it. But He does not quote all the prophecy;
He quotes only that which refers to them; what
refers to Himself He keeps in His own mind.
For what said the Prophet? These are his words:
"And they shall say to Him: What are these

25

wounds in the midst of Thy hands? And He shall say: With these I was wounded in the house of them that loved me. Awake, O sword, against My shepherd, and against the man that cleaveth to Me, saith the Lord of hosts: strike the Shepherd, and the sheep will be scattered, and I will turn My hand to the little ones." But after that the Prophet promises a refining of the people; and Our Lord will do no less. He says nothing of punishment; He will not retaliate; He looks beyond to the reconciliation: "But after I shall be risen again, I will go before you into Galilee."

Summary

1. Our Lord held this formal leave-taking, with all together, and with each individually, the best and the worst.

2. They were full of consolations, but also of self-confidence, which needed to be checked.

3. Yet this warning was one of sympathy, and even as He gave it, He still looked to the reunion.

II.—THE PROTESTS OF LOYALTY

"But Peter answering said to Him: Although all men shall be scandalized in Thee, I will never be scandalized. And Jesus saith to him: Amen I say to thee, today, even in this night, before the cock crow twice, thou shalt deny Me thrice. But Peter spoke the more vehemently, and said to Him: Although I should die together with Thee, I will not deny Thee. And in like manner also said they all."
—Matt. xxvi. 33-35; Mark xiv. 29-31.

1. It is natural that Peter should take alarm at this warning of Our Lord. Whatever other

26

follies and mistakes he had made in his life, however much he had hitherto been rebuked, he had never been unfaithful. On the contrary, he was Peter, and no longer Simon, precisely because he had been the first to proclaim: "Thou art the Christ, the Son of the living God." On another occasion, when so many turned away "and walked with Him no more"; when the broken-hearted Christ turned to His disciples and asked them: "Will you also leave Me?" he had spoken for them all: "Lord, to whom shall we go? Thou hast the words of eternal life." Again, on the Sea of Galilee he had walked upon the waters to his Master; and on Mount Thabor he had said in his enthusiasm: "Lord, it is good for us to be here." Never yet had he failed one tittle in his allegiance; surely, then, he would be confident now. He would be; no matter what might happen to the rest: "Although all men shall be scandalized in Thee, I will never be scandalized."

2. What do Our Lord and St. Peter mean by this being "scandalized"? We have it best expressed by the two disciples on the way to Emmaus. "We hoped," they said together, "that it was He that should have redeemed Israel." We hoped! and they were disappointed. We hoped in this "Prophet, mighty in word and work before God and all the people." They had seen all He had done, they had heard all He had said. They had trusted in Him as the Savior

of the world, as the King of Israel. And yet that was to happen this night and next day which was to shake their confidence. Before midnight they were to think less well of Him whom they had chosen for their Ideal and their Master. They were to be disillusioned and to doubt; this was to be scandalized in Him. And the same has been ever since. Jesus Christ is a disappointment to many; He is too lowly for their liking; He will not act when they think He ought. They forget His warning: "Blessed is he that shall not be scandalized in Me."

3. It cannot be doubted that these men loved Our Lord. It cannot be doubted that when they protested they meant every word they said. Perhaps it was on this account that Our Lord seemed already to have forgiven them; the seriousness of the offense seems scarcely to be noticed. Still, their love was not enough to save them from disaster. Their spirit may indeed have been willing, but their nature was weak; and there are times when spirit and nature must be strong together if one is to conquer. Natural virtue may usually be equal to natural trial; but man is more than merely natural, and he is submitted to more than merely natural forces. When that time comes, there must be in him something supernatural that he may come through safe; and this is the meaning of the spiritual life, the significance of prayer as a safeguard in temptation.

Summary

1. The protest of Peter seemed naturally justified. He had not yet learned himself.

2. To be "scandalized" is to be disappointed, disillusioned, grow mistrustful.

3. And they were scandalized, not because they did not love, because they had not the spiritual sight that was needed.

III.—THE BEGINNINGS OF SORROW

"Then Jesus came with them to a country place, a farm, which is called Gethsemani. And He said to His disciples: Sit you here, till I go yonder and pray. Pray, lest ye enter into temptation. And taking with Him Peter, and James and John the two sons of Zebedee, He began to grow sorrowful and to be sad, to fear and to be heavy. Then He saith to them: My soul is sorrowful even unto death; stay you here and watch with me."—Matt. xxvi. 36-38; Mark xiv. 32-34; Luke xxii. 40.

1. Three distinct stages are noticeable as Our Lord climbs the hill of Olivet. First, at the foot of the hill He leaves the main body of the Apostles. Judas is already absent; three He takes further with Him; the eight He bids sit and wait, as He had probably bade them often enough before, while He goes as usual for His evening meditation in the Garden. But this night He adds a word of warning. While they sit and wait they must "pray, lest they enter into temptation." The Blessed Sacrament will not of itself save them; their own protestations will

29

not save them; in a very short time the mob will be on them and they will run away. They have had their warning; let them take heed. There is nothing strange in this. How often has it happened to all of us that we have foreseen a crisis of great danger, and the very foresight of it has prompted us to prepare for it by prayer. Sometimes we have listened to the prompting, and have come through safely; sometimes we have not, and have been scandalized."

2. Then He climbs the hill with the three chosen companions, the companions on Thabor, the companions in the government of the Church that was to be; if companions in glory, companions also in sorrow, which has always been the lot of the faithful rulers of God's people. In their presence He lets Himself break down; this is the first step in their temptation, and He knows they will not falter, though for some of the others it might have been too much. St. Matthew and St. Mark use four words to describe this first collapse: sorrow, sadness, fear, heaviness. Perhaps we may paraphrase them thus: sense of utter failure, sense of black depression, sense of physical unnerving, sense of gloom and foreboding—those four agonies which beset every broken soul. And these were not only in His heart, but this time appeared to the three in His eyes, in His face, in His whole behavior.

3. Sometimes, in the company of a true friend,

there is sanctity in revealing one's heart. For friendship means equality, and equality demands that we should share all that we have, the sorrows with the joys. "Come to Me all you that labor and are burdened, and I will refresh you," He had said on one occasion; it was now His turn to be burdened and to need refreshment. His manner compels Him to speak, for their sake as much as for His own; He must explain His strange behavior. He is beaten, He can scarcely support Himself, He never needed a companion more than now. He knows that His only support can be in prayer, yet He feels that even for this He must have the companionship of others. "My soul is sorrowful even unto death: it would gladly die; to live as it is now is worse than to die, it is living death. Stay you here: do not leave Me"—as a dying man begs not to be left alone—"and watch with Me: just be present with Me."

Summary

1. First the eight were left, warned of danger, and warned to prepare for it.
2. Then the chosen three are permitted to witness His first agony.
3. To whom He confesses His depression and His need of a companion.

31

IV.—THE FIRST PRAYER

"And when He had gone forward a little, and was withdrawn away from them a stone's cast, kneeling down, He fell flat on the ground upon His face; and He prayed, saying: Father, if Thou wilt, remove this chalice from Me, nevertheless not My will but Thine be done. O My Father, if it is possible, let this chalice pass from Me. Nevertheless not as I will but as Thou wilt. Abba, Father, all things are possible to Thee. Take away this chalice from Me. But not what I will, but what Thou wilt."—Matt. xxvi. 36-39; Mark xiv. 32-36; Luke xxii. 40-42.

1. Here the first phase of the Passion begins. Before any man has yet touched Him, before any wound has been inflicted on Him, we find Our Lord more broken by suffering than we shall see Him during the whole course of the Passion. Here He appears as a broken man; we shall not see that again; on the contrary, as we shall have reason again and again to recall, His very independence and unbrokenness is perhaps the chief feature of the rest of the story. But here He is bowed down: He falls, first to His knees, then flat on His face upon the ground. Such scenes, of men broken by whatever sorrow, are always terrible; this surpasses them all. Let it be remembered that in this, and throughout the whole Passion, there is no pretending. Our Lord suffered that which brought His humanity to such a pass. We wonder what it could have been; St. Paul gives

the key: "Christ loved me, and gave Himself for me."

2. But can we go no deeper? Can we with any certainty analyze the ingredients of the chalice which He so abhorred? It could not have been merely a fear of the coming Passion; it is impossible to believe that Our Lord would pray so vehemently against that which, on other occasions, He had even said He desired. But if we have ever felt remorse at some shameful thing we have done, if we have ever shared the shame of another by receiving some of the blame or the stain of his misdeeds—a relation, a friend, a disciple, with whom we have been connected, or for whom we have been responsible—then we may understand a little, a very little, of the shame of Him who had made Himself man, who had shared all with man, who in consequence took upon Himself the burden of man's evil, who felt it equally with man—nay, more than man, since He alone could comprehend the meaning of sin, who, as it were, that night felt Himself guilty, not of one sin, nor of one man's sins, but of all the sins of all the world. The sense of guilt has driven men to madness, to suicide; it is the ingredient of Hell, in this world and in the next. Then, what must that agony have been of Him who for man was, as St. Paul tells us, "made sin"!

3. This, then, was the agony He would have removed "if it were possible." He appeals with

33

a kind of protest. "Father!—O My Father!—Abba, Father!"—He cries out, as if the claim of Sonship should be enough. Had it not been enough for the Prodigal Son in the parable, and was He not, even if He had taken upon Himself all the sins of all men, still the very Son of His Father? But there was something else to be considered. The Father loved His Son dearly; but He also loved mankind. The Son loved the Father dearly; but He, too, dearly loved mankind. And on this account that the chalice should be removed was not possible; for then love would never have been satisfied.

Summary

1. Our Lord is here more bent beneath His burden than in any other scene of the Passion.
2. The content of that burden was mainly all the sins of all mankind.
3. The prayer was genuine; but love made it that it could not be heard.

V.—THE SLEEPING APOSTLES

"And He cometh to His disciples and findeth them asleep. And He saith to Peter: Simon, sleepest thou? What! Couldst thou, could you, not watch one hour with Me? Watch ye and pray that ye enter not into temptation. The spirit indeed is willing but the flesh is weak."—Matt. xxvi. 40-41; Mark xiv. 37, 38.

1. The affection and the tender feeling seen in Our Lord's coming back to His disciples in the midst of His agony is a touch of human

34

nature that is surely not surpassed in the whole Bible. "I looked for one that would weep together with Me, and there was none; for one that would comfort Me, and I found none." He went, not so much for their sakes as for His own. It was a perfect act of friendship. He was sharing the burden of man. He looked for man to share His burden in return, if only by compassion. Who, then, shall say after this that to seek relief in distress from those from whom true friendship gives us the right to seek it is a weakness? Or if it is a weakness, then it is one not inconsistent with the perfect imitation of Our Lord. "A brother helped by a brother is like a strong city"; and of the two, there is rather too little mutual support in this world than too much. Let us not, then, too easily condemn it: for "as often as you do it to the least, you do it to Me."

2. But though to seek comfort when in need and to find it is a perfect thing, to seek it and not to find it may be the occasion of still greater perfection. And this was the lot of Our Lord on this terrible night. "He came unto His own and His own received Him not," is St. John's summary of Our Lord's life; when he wrote those words, had he in his mind that night when he himself slept at the gate of the Garden? His own had no comfort for Him. But He was not angered; He was only disappointed—only disappointed! as He had been many a time

before, as He has been many a time since. And
His disappointment did not harden Him against
them; it only made Him feel for them the more.
He did not think of His own loss; He thought
only of what they were losing. So it is with
true friendship; if we are truly another's friend,
and he hurts us, we are sorry more for him
than for ourselves.

3. This is the first suffering of the Passion,
the neglect of His own, and we may well ask
ourselves whether it has not been put first with
a special object. In His lifetime the neglect of
men was the only thing of which He complained;
since His leaving this world we may safely say
that nothing else has given Him more to endure.
For those who know no better there is excuse
enough; for His enemies there is separate treatment; but for His own, for those who have
accepted His livery in Baptism, who have been
fed upon His Body and Blood, who have been
sanctified at every fresh turning of their lives
by the sacraments, who look for His welcome
at the hour of death, who appreciate all or much
of the wonderful things He has done for them
during life—for how many of these does Our
Lord's rebuke hold good: "Sleepest thou?" Do
you not care? "Could you not watch one hour?"
Is My company, even for an hour at a time,
too much? "Watch and pray, that ye enter not
into temptation." If you will not help yourselves
I cannot help you. "The spirit is willing, but

36

the flesh is weak." Without Me you can do nothing; with Me there is nothing you cannot do.

Summary

1. Our Lord was a true friend, in weakness as well as in strength.
2. "He came unto His own, and His own received Him not."
3. And the same is still too true today.

VI.—THE SECOND PRAYER

"And going away again, He went the second time, and prayed, saying the selfsame words: O My Father, if this chalice cannot pass except I drink it, Thy will be done. And He cometh again and findeth them asleep; for their eyes were heavy with sorrow. And He said to them: Why sleep you? Arise, pray, lest you enter into temptation. And they knew not what to answer Him."—Matt. xxvi. 42, 43; Mark xiv. 39, 40; Luke xxii. 45, 46.

1. Undoubtedly the first ingredient of Our Lord's cup of sorrow was the sense of the sin of the world, the sense that in some way it was His own, the sense that in Him it was to be expiated. But this was intensified by many others. There was the intensity of His love. The more we care for others, the more we suffer for them and with them; what, then, must have been the measure of the suffering of Our Lord for us? Again, there was the determination that He would not be outdone in generosity; safely, then, we may say that the greatest sufferer in

37

the world does but approach to the suffering of Our Lord. Again, there was the fact of His refined and perfect nature. The more perfect the creature, the more keenly does it feel; what, then, was the suffering of the nature of Our Lord?

2. In these and countless other ways may we grow in the understanding of the Agony in the Garden, considering only the perfection of His human nature. There is yet another, of which we human beings can only catch a glimpse; it is contained in that word "Abba, Father." For if He could be so broken at the thought of man, because He loved man, because He was Himself Man, because man had done so ill, what must have been His agony, His amazement, on the side of God, when He thought of God His Father, whom man had defied; when He thought of Himself, God the Son, whom man had so ignored, and was soon to do to death; when He felt His love for the Father so insulted well up within Him, and the love of the Father encompass Him all about? We human beings can only guess at the meaning of all this. We try to express it by the term "the wrath of God," and speak of it as being visited on Our Lord. But we mean almost the opposite; we mean the love of God unrequited, insulted, the love of God devouring Our Lord, so to speak, in its effort to win back the love of man. Whatever language we use must always seem extravagant,

for we are dealing with a love, and therefore a suffering, which human words can never express.

3. Lastly, there was His own part in this drama. It was an increase of agony to Himself that His Sacred Humanity should meet with so much ingratitude, and neglect, and forgetfulness. It was an increase of agony to know that for so many His sufferings were to bear so little fruit; that while He was to be for the resurrection of many, there were also many for whom He was to be the fall. It was an increase of agony to know that in His mystical Body, the Church, the Passion was to be continued; that not only "this night," but through all time, man would be scandalized in Him through her, men would take offense because of her seeming weakness. It was an increase of agony to foresee the treatment He would receive in His Sacramental Life, the insults through all time.

Summary

1. We must measure Our Lord's agony by the perfection of His Human nature.

2. We must measure it by the perfection of His love for His Father.

3. We must measure it by the personal sufferings He could not forget in Himself.

VII.—THE SWEAT OF BLOOD

"And leaving them, He went away again, and He prayed the third time, saying the same words. And there appeared to Him an Angel from Heaven, strengthening Him. And being in an agony, He prayed the longer. And His sweat became as drops of blood trickling down upon the ground. Then He cometh the third time to His disciples and saith to them: Sleep ye on now and take your rest. It is enough, the hour is come. Behold the hour is at hand, and the Son of Man shall be betrayed into the hands of sinners. Rise up, let us go; behold he that will betray Me is at hand."—Matt. xxvi. 44-46; Mark xiv. 41, 42; Luke xxii. 45, 46.

1. There is something very becoming in this picture of consolation which is told us by St. Luke. In the trial of the Angels, before the beginning of man, many had been faithful; they had bowed before the Man-God that was to be. When the time was full, an Angel announced His coming; when He came, and man took no notice of Him, the skies were thronged with angels singing His glory. When He lay in the desert, exhausted in body, tempted by the devil, "Behold Angels came and ministered unto Him." We do not wonder, then, that this third time, when again He is deserted by man, and tempted by Satan, an Angel is visible at His side, and gives Him the succor that as Man He needs.

2. Thus is Our Lord's prayer heard. But let us notice, the answer to the prayer is very different from the words of the petition. He

40

asked that the chalice might be removed; instead, it is made yet more bitter, by the continued neglect of His chosen three, by the coming ever nearer of the traitor and his band, by His own growing weakness and inability to resist. But there comes along with all this, not mere comfort, but increase of strength; not relief from His burden, but the power to endure yet more; not an end to the agony, but the courage to "pray the longer"; not rest at last upon the soft grass, but "resistance even unto blood," so that "His sweat became as drops of blood trickling on the ground." Is there anything more sublime, and yet more human, than that blood-bathed Body? So does God hear prayer; so much farther does God see than we. When we ask for rest, for consolation, He prefers to make us heroes; and when it is over, and we look back, we thank Him that "not our will, but His has been done." There is no exception to this rule.

3. What a transformation takes place after this third prayer! To the end of the Passion, no matter what men may do to Him, we shall never see Him falter or broken any more. Always henceforth He is Master. He has strength for Himself, except such as may depend upon His poor worn body, and He has strength for everyone about Him. His disciples may sleep if they will; He will protect them; in the hour of danger He will call them. The hour does

come; He does call them; He gives them fair warning; He recommends them to go; there is strength in every word and gesture. We look on amazed; we wonder whether we have understood aright; and yet around us we see the same illustrated in those who seek their own support in prayer.

Summary

1. The coming of the Angel is of a piece with the rest of the life of Our Lord.

2. His prayer is heard, not in the letter, but with an increase of strength.

3. And that strength is abiding, not for Himself only, but also for others.

VIII.—JUDAS AND HIS FOLLOWERS

"Now Judas also, who betrayed Him, one of the twelve, knew the place, because Jesus had often resorted thither together with His disciples. Judas therefore, having received a band of men and servants from the chief priests and the Pharisees, the scribes and the ancients of the people, cometh thither while He was yet speaking, and with him a great multitude, with lanterns and torches and weapons, swords and clubs and staves."—Matt, xxvi. 47; Mark xiv. 43; Luke xxii. 47; John xviii. 2, 3.

1. It is almost terrible to notice how the Evangelists linger on the name of Judas. Apart from other places in the Gospels where he is mentioned, and where the Evangelists give him the distinguishing epithet of "the traitor," here St. Matthew, St. Mark, and St. Luke call him "Judas, one of the twelve," and John calls him "Judas, who betrayed Him." The personal shame

of having him among their number is felt by all four. It is the shame of a family when a son or a brother or a sister has disgraced himself or herself, and therefore all the rest; the shame of a priest when he hears of a brother-priest having done something unworthy of his calling, but, of course, incalculably deeper. They seem to be reminding themselves of the duty of atonement that belongs to the rest because of the treachery of one; the zeal they must put forward to prove to Our Lord that the rest at least are faithful.

2. At the same time they seem to be reminding themselves that if one such as he may fall so low, others may do likewise. He was one of the carefully chosen twelve; therefore he possessed at the beginning the qualities that would make a saint, he was given the training that should have made a saint; from first to last he had the special affection of Our Lord. He was entrusted with the materialities of the Apostolic body, therefore he possessed gifts of nature qualifying him for this post; he had in consequence a greater experience than the others among men, which some seem to think so valuable in the making of an Apostle. And yet he fell; his very promotion brought about his fall; had he been kept in the background he might never have been tempted, "Howl, thou fir-tree, for the cedar has fallen!" As St. Paul wrote long afterwards: "I chastise my body, and bring

43

it into subjection, lest while preaching to others I myself become a castaway."

3. Then there is the multitude: the people whom Our Lord had cured; the people for whom He had toiled unceasingly; the people dear to His heart; the people who, the Sunday before, had cried "Hosanna to the Son of David"; "a great multitude," say two Evangelists, with "a band of men and servants," says St. John; from "the chief priests and ancients of the people," says St. Matthew; from "the chief priests and the scribes and the ancients," says St. Mark; "from the chief priests and Pharisees," says St. John. The scene is unmistakable. What a growth of cockle among the wheat, and how quickly had it sprung up! All in four short days, the four days of Our Lord's hardest work on earth, the four days in which, as never before, He had vindicated His cause and put His enemies to silence. It was a proof that He had failed— He so eloquent, He so genuine, He so deserving of success, who fought besides, not for Himself, but for His Father, and for the very people who had here gathered against Him! Such is the wisdom of the multitude.

Summary

1. The shame of the other Apostles because of the treachery of Judas.

2. The fall of Judas, from what; by what means, to what it came.

3. The multitude, for whom Our Lord had done so much.

44

IX.—THE HOMAGE OF THE ENEMY

"Jesus, therefore, knowing all things that were to come upon Him, went forward and saith to them; Whom seek ye? They answered Him: Jesus of Nazareth. Jesus saith to them: I am He. And Judas also who betrayed Him stood with them. As soon, then, as He had said to them: I am He, they went backward and fell to the ground. Again, therefore, He asked them: Whom seek ye? And they said: Jesus of Nazareth. Jesus answered: I have told you that I am He. If therefore you seek Me, let these go their way; that the word might be fulfilled which He said: Of them whom Thou hast given Me I have not lost any one."—John xviii. 4-9.

1. This scene is given to us only by St. John. St. John on more than one occasion has been careful to emphasize the fact that Our Lord knew what was about to happen. He keeps us in mind that Our Lord was always God, even at the moments when He permitted His weak human nature to be uppermost. Other Saints have found deep matter for meditation in this thought—St. Augustine, Ludolph of Saxony, St. Ignatius Loyola, Fra Thomas of Jesus, and others. It is as though, while the panorama of the Passion moves before them, they keep saying to themselves: "And this is God all the time!" We may well repeat the same, at any hour, but especially now when we look at Our Lord, broken and blood-bespattered, yet erect and commanding, for the first time confronting His enemies.

45

THE CROWN OF SORROW

2. "Erect and commanding." Now begins that characteristic dignity which never leaves Our Lord throughout the Passion. He confronts them; they are cowed and silent, as a coward is silent when true strength confronts it. He is the first to speak; and His words now, at the beginning of the end—how strange!—are the same as when He first appeared. "Whom seek ye?" He asked the first disciples when they followed Him down the river-side. "Master, where do You live?" was their answer. "Come and see," He said; and that was His first gathering. Now, how different! Yet He will have His name proclaimed even if it be by His enemies. They shall say definitely at the outset who is their object of hatred: "Jesus of Nazareth." That name will be heard again in the next few days. It will be seen on Calvary. It will be heard and seen, the abiding object of hatred, but also "the power of God and the glory of God," as long as the world shall last.

3. "Wherefore God hath exalted Him above the highest, and hath bestowed on Him the name which is above every name; that at the name of Jesus every knee should bend in Heaven, on earth, and that every tongue should confess that Jesus Christ is Lord, to the glory of God the Father." Had St. Paul this scene in mind when he wrote this triumphant sentence? "I am He," He had said to the Samaritan woman, and had converted her. "Fear not, it is

I," He had said to the disciples on the water; and they had been calmed. "Before Abraham was, I am," was His thundering refutation of His enemies. And later, when all the trouble is over, He will come again and say to His own: "Fear not, it is I"; and with the same word, "It is I, Jesus," He will turn the persecutor Saul into St. Paul. There is indeed great courage for us all in this word: *Ego sum,* I am He.

Summary

1. St. John emphasizes the Divine nature in the midst of the human weakness.

2. "Whom seek ye?"—"Jesus of Nazareth." The commanding, the stamp set on the Passion.

3. The effect of Our Lord's answer: "I am He," then and at all times.

X.—THE BETRAYAL

"And he that betrayed Him had given them a sign, saying: Whomsoever I shall kiss, that is He; lay hold on Him, hold Him fast, and lead Him away cautiously. And when he was come, immediately going up to Jesus, he said: Hail, Rabbi, and he kissed Him. And Jesus said to him: Friend, whereto art thou come? Judas, dost thou betray the Son of Man with a kiss? Then they came up, and laid hands on Jesus, and held him."—Matt. xxvi. 48-50; Mark xiv. 44-46; Luke xxii. 48.

1. It has been said by some, as a sort of defense of poor Judas, that he hoped by this

act of betrayal to give Our Lord an opportunity of vindicating Himself before the people; that he had grown tired of this long waiting for the Kingdom of God to come, and intended, as it were, to compel Him at last to show His power and declare Himself. But the wording of the text does not seem to give much sanction to this theory. At the beginning we are distinctly told that Judas had at last come to prefer silver and gold to Jesus Christ; he made a deliberate choice between two alternatives, and bartered one for the other. Again, Our Lord's dealing with Judas in the Supper-room shows deep hardness of heart; it is hard to believe that Judas did not know that Our Lord understood. Finally, here the fear of Judas is, not that the treachery should succeed, but that it should fail. He takes every precaution, and, to make himself doubly sure, he trades upon the tender affection of Our Lord, which could be counted upon to help in the betrayal rather than to frustrate it.

2. It was as if he said: "Though, Rabbi, You might save Yourself for Your own sake, yet let Yourself be captured for mine." And the greeting of Our Lord confirms this view. With the greatness of a hero, He lets things take their course. Had it been Herod, or a stranger, or the scribes and Pharisees alone, He might have resisted. He might have "passed through their midst," as He had done on a former occa-

48

sion when they wished to take His life. He
might have flogged them from before Him, as
He did that day when the zeal of His Father's
house devoured Him. He might have left them
on the ground where they had fallen. But the
traitor is His friend; the traitor is the trusted
Judas; He can only show His greatness against
Himself now, keeping down the nausea He must
have felt when the traitor's lips touched His
cheek.

3. And the multitude seem to feel the same.
It is difficult to imagine that they would not
have known Our Lord without any special notifi-
cation from the traitor.. He tells them Himself
a little later that He is perfectly well known
to them, and been among them every day of
late. They had seen Him, they had heard Him,
they had spoken with Him often enough; He
had Himself already told them who He was,
and His word was better than the word of a
traitor. But with one of His own at their head
they had a certain sense of security. If He
were inclined to touch them, He might be de-
terred from the sight of him. If they had any
doubts of their own, the traitor at their head
would seem to justify their proceedings; they
could silence their own consciences, by throwing
on him the responsibility. So the world has
hidden and clothed its malice under the name of
some traitor to Our Lord.

Summary

1. The betrayal of Our Lord would seem to have been deliberate and intentional.

2. Our Lord yields to the treachery of a friend, when He had not yielded to enemies.

3. The multitude, powerless of themselves, hid themselves beneath the traitor's name.

XI.—THE HEALING OF MALCHUS

"And they that were about Him, seeing what would follow, said to Him: Lord, shall we strike with the sword? Then one of them that was with Jesus, Simon Peter, stretching forth his hand, drew his sword, and striking the servant of the high priest, cut off his ear. And the name of the servant was Malchus. But Jesus answering said: Suffer ye thus far. Then he said to Peter: Put up again thy sword into the scabbard. For all that take the sword shall perish with the sword. Thinkest thou that I cannot ask My Father, and He will give me presently more than twelve legions of Angels? How, then, shall the Scriptures be fulfilled, that so it must be done? The chalice which My Father hath given Me, shall I not drink it? And when He had touched his ear, He healed him."—Matt. xxvi. 51-54; Mark xiv. 47-49; Luke xxii. 50, 51; John xviii. 10, 11.

1. What strange circumstances are these for the working of Our Lord's last healing miracle. Unlike all the others in the New Testament, the victim is not one whom Our Lord has met in the course of His day's work, a faithful follower, or at least one who believed in Him and appealed by the roadside; but he is an avowed enemy, he has got his wound in an unholy cause, he has received his wound from

one of Our Lord's own defenders. One wonders what kind of gratitude He received for such an act of charity. Surely something; surely the conversion of Malchus; the fact that we are given his name, as in the later case of Simon, points to his being known later to the Evangelists, and therefore to his being among the band of the faithful.

2. One wonders, too, what must have been in the mind of Peter. Poor Peter! He had sworn before to stand up for his Master in time of trouble; his Master had expressly seen to it that he brought a sword with him to the Garden. He now does stand up for Him in the best way he knows how; and in return he is rebuked and the "good" he has done is cancelled by Our Lord Himself. Surely if He could work such a miracle as this, and under circumstances such as these, He could do no more. Evidently, then, not only is the case hopeless, but the Master has decided that it shall be hopeless, and there is nothing now to be done but run away. How easily one can so decide in questions of this kind, when for His own reasons Our Lord wills that things shall go hard with us, that our well-intentioned deeds shall turn out mistakes, and that we shall be suffered to say and do nothing in our defense.

3. Meanwhile, here once again His own commanding presence is most wonderful. From beginning to end it is shown to us that if not

51

a sparrow shall fall without His Father's consent, neither shall He Himself be maltreated without His own permission at each step. He is always Master; the consciousness of it does but make His enemies rage the more. His enemies may seize Him, but they must first fall down before Him. The friend may betray Him, but he must first be shown that the Master has not been deceived. The mob may insult Him, but they shall never be able to say that to the end He has slackened in well-doing. And the deliberateness with which He acts—deliberately refusing to ask His Father, deliberately reversing the prayer He had offered in the Garden, deliberately healing the man, while the mob must pause and look on—all this is very beautiful.

Summary

1. The cure of Malchus, the last of His cures, stands alone in its circumstances.
2. The mind of Peter, failing to understand, is tottering to its fall.
3. The mind of Our Lord, always Master, always deliberately free.

XII.—THE PROTEST OF OUR LORD

"In that same hour Jesus said to the chief priests and magistrates of the Temple, and the ancients and the multitude that were come to Him: Are you come out as it were against a robber with swords and clubs and staves to apprehend me? I sat daily with you teaching in the Temple, and you did not stretch forth your hand against Me. But this is your hour

and the power of darkness. Now all this was done
that the Scriptures of the prophets might be ful-
filled. Then His disciples, leaving Him, all fled away.
And a certain young man followed Him, having a
linen cloth cast about his naked body, and they laid
hold on him. But he, casting off the linen cloth, fled
from them naked."—Matt. xxvi. 55; Mark xiv. 48-52;
Luke xxii. 52. 53.

1. Again we are struck with the combination
of strength and weakness manifested by Our
Lord. He is able to speak to all this assembly
"as one having authority," in the way He had
always done before, on the Mount, in the Temple,
on their own ground, as it were; and yet here
He is unable to do anything for Himself. He
can only permit that feature of His soul to
appear which He has never refused to show;
that special agony, even to weakness, that it
feels with every act of ingratitude. Indignity
to Him is very hard. He will complain of it
again before the Passion is over, before the
same night is spent, but He will complain of
nothing else. And with what terrible words He
concludes: "This is your hour and the power
of darkness!" It is as though He knew that
man could not of himself be so cruel. For this
he must be allied with another power.

2. How the multitude and the leaders received
His words we are not told; with conscious
shame, no doubt, hidden beneath tumult and
bravado, but with utter disregard of their significance. The world is a past master in the

art of ignoring words which it does not wish to hear. But the disciples received the words in a stranger way, though one that need not surprise us. To them they were a knell; their hopes of years had been crushed in a moment. "We hoped that this was He that would restore the kingdom to Israel"; and now he says: "This is your hour and the power of darkness." They forget the warning; they are scandalized in Him, as He said; they fly away, every single one of them, apparently even John. And yet Our Lord had prayed for them this very night as "they who have stood with Me in My temptations."

3. One asks oneself the meaning of the episode of the man in white. Many strange details must have happened in the Passion which have not been recorded; why preserve such a detail as this? St. Mark alone tells the story; some have in consequence surmised that it was he. Others have suggested St. John. But him we meet again immediately after, and the linen cloth is strange. Let us conjecture; we can do no more. The Passion was above all others a time "for the resurrection and for the fall of many in Israel." Is this one of them? Is this a case of a vocation missed because of the difficulty? Had this man stood his ground, had he in some way shared with Our Lord the agony of the moment, might we not have had yet another name to add to those of Simon of Cyrene, and

54

Veronica, and the holy women, and the penitent thief, and Joseph of Arimathea, and Nicodemus?

Summary

1. The strength and weakness of Our Lord before the multitude.

2. The desertion of the Apostles; the plausible reasons they would give.

3. The man in the linen cloth; is this another vocation lost?

XIII.—JESUS, ANNAS, CAIPHAS

"Then the band, and the tribune, and the servants of the Jews, took Jesus and bound Him. And they led Him away to Annas first, for he was father-in-law to Caiphas, who was the high priest of that year. Now Caiphas was he who had given the counsel to the Jews, that it was expedient that one man should die for the people."—John xviii. 12-14.

1. We leave to scholars the discussion of the relations between Annas and Caiphas, who the two were, why Annas is also called the high priest, and why Our Lord is taken first to him, before appearing in the lawful court. It is enough for us to know the simple facts, and to meditate upon the procession. We can follow Our Lord down that hill of Olivet, which He had ascended and descended so often, particularly of late, not only when going to and from the Garden, but in the glorious procession of Palm Sunday—it was not far from here that He had stopped that procession and burst into tears at the sight of the doomed city before

55

Him—and in His many journeys to and from
Bethany, which lay in the other valley. Many
a time, then, must Our Lord have thought of
all that would happen on that road, as He passed
along it during these last years. We watch Him
now dragged along; we remember He is "bound";
we hear the prophecy which hints that He fell
in the brook; we ask ourselves what must have
been the sight of Him that entered the city
gate on the Sunday preceding!

2. Who was this Annas? He was first of all
a Sadducee, one of those who, as St. Matthew
tells us, "say there is no resurrection," or who,
as St. Luke writes in the Acts of the Apostles,
"say there is no resurrection, neither Angel, nor
spirit"; one of those who, when they had once
tried to catch Our Lord, had been so confuted
that "the multitudes hearing it, were in admira-
tion at His doctrine"; one, therefore, who was
not likely to make much account of the hereafter,
or of Him who spoke of His own resurrection
and return. He was one who had been many
times high-priest himself, who had secured that
his sons-in-law should succeed him; one of those
who, so far as it was possible had converted
his family into a kind of Jewish royal house
which would resist any kind of intruder.

3. And who was Caiphas? He, too, was a
Sadducee; he believed in no future life, therefore, perhaps believed in no Kingdom of the

Messiah. Moreover, he was high priest of that year; into such hands had the priesthood fallen even since the days of Zachary, and the Presentation in the Temple, even during the very thirty years that Our Lord was living on the earth! And for his principles, St. John recalls the scene when, after the raising of Lazarus, the Council gathered in alarm and asked each other: "What shall we do, for this man doth many miracles?" And Caiphas answered: "You know nothing. Neither do you consider that it is expedient for you that one man should die for the people, and that the whole nation perish not." A man, then, whose principle was expediency, whose right was might.

Summary

1. The first steps in the Passion should be traced —from Olivet to the house of Annas.

2. Annas—the Saducee, the unbeliever, the maker of a false royal house.

3. Caiphas—the Saducee, the one who first "devised to put Him to death."

XIV.—THE TRIAL BEFORE ANNAS

"The high priest then asked Jesus of His disciples and of His doctrine. Jesus answered him: I have spoken openly to the world, I have always taught in the synagogue and in the Temple whither all the Jews resort, and in private I have spoken nothing. Why askest thou Me? Ask them who have heard what I have spoken to them; behold, they know what things I have said. And when He had said these things, one of the officers standing by gave Jesus a

blow, saying: Answerest Thou the high priest so?
Jesus answered him: If I have spoken ill, give testi-
mony of the evil; but if well, why strikest thou Me?
And Annas sent him bound to Caiphas, the high
priest."—John xviii. 19-24.

1. This preliminary trial still shows Our Lord
in all His dignity. He knows that Annas has
no real jurisdiction over Him; therefore He
gives him no direct answer. More than that,
Annas inquires first of Our Lord's disciples, as
if he would gladly involve them in the ruin
of their Master. Here, indeed, for us English
Catholics, is an anticipation of those attempts
at involving others by cross-examination of our
martyrs with which their records are full. But
Our Lord sets the example of a model answer.
He does not deny that He has followers; indeed,
all the world are His followers; He points to
all those who have listened to Him "in the
synagogue and the Temple"; of His very own
He says nothing; of those whom His Father
had given Him He has not lost any one.

2. The answer is exasperating, precisely because it is so true. It is triumphant, and therefore to the vanquished it appears as an imper-
tinence. So does it appear to this court. "And
when He had answered these things, one of the
officers standing by gave Jesus a blow, saying:
Answerest Thou the high priest so?" No doubt
Our Lord had been struck already since the
affair in the Garden; but this is the first blow
of His life that is recorded. We hear it fall;

we see the livid marks it leaves upon His face; we know that from henceforth those blue stripes will be there. As we look we recall the words of the greatest of heathen philosophers. When he describes his ideal of a man, he says that he will have a great heart which will endure bravely great misfortunes, will accept even shame with equanimity. But there he draws the line; he says there is one shame which no great man will accept; to accept, he says, marks a feeble soul; he will not endure to be struck in the face. Yet here Our Lord endures it! One may say with truth, that blow marks the boundary line between paganism and Christianity; the line where paganism stops and Christianity goes forward.

3. The blow has fallen; there follows a solemn silence; for the moment all there present, soldiers, and high priest, and on-lookers alike, are awed by this wanton act of shame. They feel that they have overstepped all bounds. And in the midst of the silence is heard the solemn rebuke: "If I have spoken ill, give testimony of the evil; but if well, why strikest thou Me?" But they have now waded too deep; they will not go back. They break up the assembly; they pack off the Prisoner to another court; themselves slink away like whipped curs, as a sinner slinks away when he has done a deed of shame, and in the very act his conscience rises up and rebukes him.

Summary

1. Our Lord's defense of Himself and of His own.
2. The blow He received; the dividing-line between paganism and Christianity.
3. The rebuke which followed it, making the sinner ashamed.

XV.—THE WITNESS BEFORE CAIPHAS

"But they, holding Jesus, led Him to Caiphas the high priest, and all the priests and scribes and the ancients were assembled together. And the chief priests and the whole council sought false witness for evidence against Jesus, that they might put Him to death. For though many false witnesses had come in, and bore false witness against Him their evidence did not agree. And last of all there came in two false witnesses. They, rising up, bore false witness against Him, saying: We heard Him say, I will destroy this Temple of God made with hands, and within three days, I will build another not made with hands. And their witness did not agree."—Matt. xxvi. 59-61; Mark xiv. 55-59.

1. The court of Annas was no proper court; it had no authority whatsoever; it was only something that had grown up round a man of strong will, stronger than his relatives whom he had brought into office, to whom the people had learned to pay deference as to a leader. Hence by it Our Lord had refused to be judged. He had defied it, and had been rewarded by the blow. But the court of Caiphas was lawful, even though unjust; and at once we find Our Lord treating it with deference. When it wa

60

merely brutal and false, He treated it with silence; when the lawful authority asked a lawful question, He gave it a complete answer, be the consequences what they might. As He had said on a former occasion, so He Himself did now: "Whatsoever they command you, observe and do; but according to their works do ye not."

2. The witnesses against Him were many. There will always be found in this world (1) those who will put the right in the wrong; (2) those who will give evidence that will flatter the powers that be. Everyone of us knows what it is to be misunderstood by even one; some of us may know what it is to be deliberately maligned by one, or perhaps two; but how many of us have been so maltreated as to have had many against us, who have, one and all, deliberately borne false witness, whose word has been preferred to ours, though they have clearly lied, and though they have clearly contradicted themselves and one another? Many of us have had our words misquoted against us; some have had them deliberately twisted; but how many have had our mere figures of speech turned into explicit statements, and by addition of a word here, and a subtraction of a word there, have been convicted out of our own mouths?

3. Yet this and worse is the practice played upon Our Lord. They go back to His earliest days of preaching. They pick out His greatest

prophecy. They give it their own interpretation. That interpretation is too absurd even for the Council to accept it. All the time He answered nothing. He might easily have reminded them, had He wished, of His exact words and their meaning. He might have shown them that they were themselves their own accusers; that they had understood perfectly well what He had meant, from the changes they had made in His words. Later, when He was dead and buried, they showed that they had understood from their appeal to Pilate: "This man said while He was yet alive, After three days I will rise again." But He said nothing. He would not argue with such men. To suffer at their hands was no disgrace; it is never a disgrace to suffer at such hands.

Summary

1. Our Lord evaded the question of Annas; in the court of Caiphas and Pilate He submitted.

2. The evidence against Him was such as is always against the truth, but more intense.

3. It did but prove the greater guilt of His accusers; hence He had no need to speak.

XVI.—THE CONDEMNATION BEFORE CAIPHAS

"And the high priest, rising up in the midst, asked Jesus, saying: Answerest Thou nothing to the things that are laid to Thy charge by these men? But Jesus held His peace and answered nothing. Again the high priest asked Him and said to Him: I adjure Thee, by the living God, that Thou tell us if Thou be the Christ, the Son of the blessed God. And Jesus

*said to him: Thou hast said it, I am. Nevertheless
I say to you, hereafter you shall see the Son of Man
sitting on the right hand of the power of God, and
coming in the clouds of Heaven. Then the high
priest rent his garments, saying: He hath blasphemed; what further need have we of witnesses?
Behold, now you have heard the blasphemy, what
think you? But they all answering condemned Him
and said: He is guilty of death."—Matt. xxvi. 62-66;
Mark xiv. 60-64.*

1. The witnesses did not deserve to be refuted;
their best refutation, the only refutation of such
as batten on untruth, is silence; to them, then,
Our Lord answered nothing. But Caiphas was
at least a lawful judge; and though he could
be ignored when he united himself with the
false witnesses, still, when he spoke in his own
name he had a right to be answered. Something
seemed to tell him this; there is a consciousness
of it in the words:"I adjure thee, by the living
God." He knows with whom he is dealing; he
knows that this Man will speak the truth; he
knows how exactly to word his question; he
words it as Peter worded his great confession:
"Thou art Christ, the Son of the living God."
That he should know all this is a terrible confession of faith. Of all men in the Passion,
none seems more to sin against the light than
Caiphas; so much does he seem to sin against
it that one wonders how a man could be so
audacious.

2. Caiphas knew; and he knew, therefore,
what would be the answer of Our Lord; if he

had not known, he might have suspected he might get some other answer, and that would have ruined his place. He received the answer he expected; but he received something more. Yes, Jesus was the Christ, the Son of the living God. And therefore the time would come when the tables would be turned; when He, not Caiphas, would be the judge; when the mystery of Heaven, not the glamor of this court, would surround Him; and He recalls the description He had elsewhere given of His coming at the end of the world. Let it be noticed that this is the first time in Scripture that Our Lord is heard to state so explicitly that He is "Christ, the Son of the living God."

3. Then came the ending, and the universal condemnation. What can have been in the minds of the Council? Either they believed His words or they did not. If they did not believe that He was what He declared Himself to be, then they might indeed have had Him put to death, but at the same time they could only have treated Him as one who was mad—as Herod treated Him, for instance, who was incapable of faith. Only a madman could have made such a claim, especially in such circumstances. But they did not laugh Him to scorn; they did not ridicule; they took Him seriously, bitterly; they "did protest too much"; and their cry, "He is guilty of death," can only be taken as their own terrible death sentence.

Summary

1. The solemn adjuration of Caiphas seems to prove that he knew the truth.

2. Our Lord answers, and for the first time says explicitly that He is God.

3. The Council condemns; their sentence is their own condemnation.

XVII.—FIRST DENIAL OF PETER

"But Simon Peter followed Jesus afar off, and so did another disciple, to the high priest's palace. And that disciple was known to the high priest, and went in with Jesus into the court of the high priest. But Peter stood at the door without. Then the other disciple, who was known to the high priest, went out and spoke to the portress and brought in Peter. And when they had kindled a fire of coals in the midst of the hall, because it was cold, and were sitting about it, Peter sat with the servants to see the end, and warmed himself. Now when Peter was in the court below, there cometh one of the maidservants of the high priest, the maid that was portress; and when she had seen Peter sitting in the light and warming himself, and had looked on him, she said: Thou also wast with Jesus of Nazareth, the Galilaean. This man also was with him. Art not thou also one of this man's disciples? But he denied Him before them all, saying: Woman, I am not. I know Him not. I neither know nor understand what thou sayest."—Matt. xxvi. 69, 70; Mark xiv. 66-68; Luke xxii. 54-57; John xviii. 25.

[NOTE.—There is, perhaps, no scene in Scripture more difficult to harmonize than the scene of Peter's first denial; yet, as usual where harmony is difficult, the fact itself cannot for a moment be suspected. The first three Evan-

gelists give it at the fireside, and do not say
that the maid who challenged Peter was portress.
St. John seems to imply that the denial took
place at the gate as soon as Peter had entered,
and that it was made in answer to a challenge
of the portress. If, as seems to be right, we
must confine the denials to three, it would appear
to be necessary to give the preference to the
account of St. Matthew, St. Mark, and St. Luke,
and to take from St. John further details. At
the same time, it is to be noted that St. John
puts the second denial at the fireside, which the
others place after he had left it; the third he
describes as in answer to "the kinsman of him
whose ear Peter cut off," whom the others do
not mention. The narrative of St. John is
throughout much more circumstantial and dramatic than is that of the others. It reads much
more like the evidence of an eyewitness; it is
written by one who already knew the other
accounts; and if, as many suppose, St. John
was "the other disciple known to the high
priest," it may well be the most accurate version.
If we allowed four denials, then the accounts
could be easily reconciled—one at the gate, one
at the fireside, and two after Peter had left it;
though here, again, it is not clear that all are
speaking of the same occasions. But for the
purposes of meditation we have preferred the
traditional three; the solemn fact remains, and
alone concerns us.]

1. Peter had had his warning; he had disbelieved in it; he had despised it; a later word implies that he had forgotten it; in consequence even Peter, the first to declare Our Lord to be "the Christ, the Son of the living God," is the first to deny Him.

2. The reason for the fall is clear. It is not merely fear of the portress; had they been alone, would he have denied Our Lord at her taunt? Would she ever have uttered it? Rather it is that demoralizing influence of a crowd, of public opinion, close akin to human respect, which so often seems to paralyze our lips when we would speak the truth.

3. And the occasion is no less clear. Peter's motive for going was good; he went "that he might see the end." But the motive was not enough to justify his being there. He forgot the prayer: "Lead us not into temptation."

Summary

1. The neglect of warning.
2. The reason of the fall.
3. The occasion.

XVIII.—THE FURTHER DENIALS OF PETER

"And he went forth before the court, out of the gate, and the cock crew. And again another maidservant saw him, and she began to say to the standers-by: This is one of them. This man also was with Jesus of Nazareth. Thou also art one of them. And again he denied with an oath: O man, I am not. I do not know the man. And after a little

67

while, about the space of one hour after, they that
stood by came again and said to Peter: surely thou
also art one of them, for even thy speech doth dis-
cover thee. Thou also art a Galilaean. And another
man, one of the servants of the high priest, a kins-
man to him whose ear Peter cut off, saith to him:
Did I not see thee in the Garden with Him? Then
he began to curse and swear that he knew not the
man, saying: Man, I know not what thou sayest; I
know not this man of whom you speak."—Matt. xxvi.
71-74; Mark xiv. 69-71; Luke xxii. 58-60, John xviii.
26, 27.

1. Peter has been sufficiently disturbed by his
first denial to become restless; it is with that
restlessness which is peculiar to the first conscious sense of having done wrong. He has
got up and left the group with an air of offended
innocence, and the group has followed him with
a leer of unaffected contempt. It has not been
deceived by the denial; but it triumphs over
both the denier and the Denied. He knows they
are not convinced; and they are happy at the
thought that this Jesus of Nazareth cannot
after all, be very much, since His followers so
easily deny Him and betray Him. If these made
so little of Him, others could not be expected
to do more.

2. Meanwhile, Peter meets another maid, a-
nother of the type that is always on the side
of the crowd, as is the worst of those who seek
for notice at any cost. She has no respect for
him. She has her own end to gain, and has
only her tongue with which to gain it. So she

stabs and stabs, and thinks herself triumphant when her victim turns. And the poor victim, how he turns! First, to the tribunal: "Man, I know Him not!" And of what is he accused? Of being a friend of Jesus Christ! And what does he deny? "I know not the man!" The Man! Him whom but a short time before he had called "Christ, the Son of the living God"! And all this he confirms with an oath. He must conform with the usages of his surroundings and practice their speech. So strong is the silent influence of evil company on us, no matter who we be, no matter how carefully guarded. How often do we hear it said, "If others would leave us alone it would be easy to avoid evil doing."

3. It is an hour after. In a crisis such as this an hour is a long time. Did the trial of Our Lord, then, even before the spitting and the buffeting began, take so long? What could they have been doing with Him all that time? For Peter, too, an hour in that crowd was a long time. What had he been doing? He had not been standing there silent, that is clear. He had talked enough for the by-standers to detect that he came from Galilee; his speech betrayed him. Perhaps he had said enough to remind the servants of him in the Garden; for Peter was always impetuous, and unguarded in his speech. The evidence was overwhelming. The poor man had gone so far, he could not and would not draw back. He would only repeat

his crime; it was easier now than at first; having sinned twice, the third was almost spontaneous.

Summary

1. The effect of Peter's first denial, on the audience and on himself.
2. The second denial: its occasion, the temptress, its kind.
3. The third denial: the hour's interval, the occasion, the ease of the fall.

XIX.—THE CONVERSION OF PETER

"And immediately, while he was yet speaking, the cock crew again. And the Lord, turning, looked on Peter. And Peter remembered the word that the Lord Jesus had said to him: Before the cock crow twice thou shalt deny Me thrice. And Peter went out, and began to weep, and wept bitterly."—Matt. xxvi. 75; Mark xiv. 72; Luke xxii. 61, 62; John xviii. 27.

1. It should not be difficult to spend an hour in contrition with Peter; if we would enter into his heart, let us enter into our own, joining our own offense with his, realizing how little has been our provocation compared with his, and yet how near to his has been our downfall; not so dramatic, perhaps, but has it not been just as despicable? We have had our warning and we have ignored it; we have had our occasion and we have risked it; we have fallen once with an effort, but the second and third

70

offenses have come more easily; in the midst of our wrong-doing the crowing of the cock has been heard, but we have hardened ourselves and gone on. It is the tale of every sin. There is always some excuse. We blame our circumstances; but how often are we not obliged to say that, in spite of them, the fault is all our own?

2. "And the Lord, turning, looked on Peter." It is a shock to discover that Our Lord had been there all the time. Peter had denied his Master, not behind His back, not in a distant place, but within His sight, perhaps even within hearing. "He saved others, Himself He cannot save," not even from such insult as this. And yet, with what effect! In the days gone by, when Jesus and His disciples were passing through Samaria, some people mocked them; and the disciples in their indignation begged of Him to call down fire from Heaven and destroy them. But He did not; He merely reminded them of mercy. If, then, they had been heard, what now might poor Peter have expected? For surely this denial cancelled his former confession of faith; this association with His enemies cancelled his vocation to the Apostolate; this weakness before a servant-girl made him for ever unfit to be called "the rock." Yet what did he receive? A look, a look of love; a look of love mingled with a little reproach; perhaps the lips moved and he caught the words "Peter—friend!" as the traitor had heard "Judas—friend!" in

71

the Garden; but not a sign of bitterness, or of anger, or of intention to retaliate.

3. "And Peter remembered." To think that he could ever have forgotten! And yet we know ourselves how blinding, how deafening, sin can be. In the midst of the fascination all warnings are forgotten, all resolutions ignored—till all is over, and the cry of conscience, "What hast thou done?" rings in our ears and tears our hearts. Now he remembered. He remembered the warning. He remembered the love with which it had been uttered. He remembered the Communion, the washing of the feet, the broken Heart of that evening. He remembered all the Master had done for him, all He had given him, all the confidence He had placed in him. He remembered his own enthusiastic affection, his great desires. He remembered all his past failures and the way they had been met. "And he began to weep." When will the tears cease?

Summary

1. We can enter into Peter's heart best by entering into our own.
2. The Lord, turning, looked on Peter.
3. Peter remembered, and began to weep.

XX.—THE INSULTS BEFORE CAIPHAS

"And the men that held Him began to spit in His face, and mocked Him, and buffeted Him. And they blindfolded Him and covered His face, and smote Him in the face, and the servants struck Him with the palms of their hands. And they asked Him, saying: Prophesy unto us, O Christ, who is he that struck Thee? And many other things, blaspheming, they said against Him."—Matt. xxvi. 67, 68; Mark xiv. 65; Luke xxii. 63-65.

1. In a sense this scene is the climax of the Passion. To a sensitive man of honor like Our Lord whatever came after could have been as nothing compared with this hour of supreme insult. And our own instinct through the ages has told us that this is of all the scenes in the Passion the most dreadful, since art has attempted to idealize all the others, but not this. The Agony, the Betrayal, the Trial, the Scourging, the Crowning, the Crucifixion, the Funeral —all these have been the subjects of great masterpieces; but has any artist made an ideal picture of "the men that held Him began to spit in His face"? Yet so it was; and the great and respectable scribes and Pharisees looked on, and said not a word, perhaps forgot themselves so far as to join in the spitting; for nothing so reduces a man to the level of a savage as hatred. We can only look on dumbfounded, repeating: "They spat in His face; they spat in His face."

73

2. Then follows the series of insults, with an ingenuity of invention which only devilry can display. They spat in His face. They mimicked His every movement. His dignity they mocked as pride; His silence they mocked as if He were dumb; His compassion they mocked as sourness or weakness. making wry faces hanging down their mouths. They cuffed Him; they kicked Him; in their desire to out-rival each other, as is the universal custom of a persecuting mob, they invent strange abuses of His body on the spur of the moment. They tied a rag about His eyes. It is something at least to be able to see one's enemy and tormentor; but to be prevented from this, not to know whence the blows are coming, or what will be next—the agony of it! They smote Him in the face, an insult which—as we have said elsewhere—if accepted without remonstrance, in the eyes of the world proves a mean fellow, a coward. And all this He endured without a word.

3. Last of all they insulted His divinity. On other occasions He had shown supernatural knowledge; there were those present who knew it, or they would never have recalled it now; let Him show it again. He had proclaimed Himself before the Anointed, the Messiah; let Him prove it now. "He has saved others, Himself He cannot save." The confession of the truth, of deep-down belief in all the evidence, rings through the whole tale of its defiance, just as

the most savage persecution is usually a confession that the persecutors know that they are wrong. They "do protest too much"; they substitute might for right; men do not use such violence to destroy a thing in which they have no faith. The love of Our Lord cannot go lower down than this. He has Himself said that "Greater love no man hath than that he lay down his life for his friend"; but what are we to say of this total surrender of honor?

Summary

1. This scene is the climax of insult.
2. Then follows a series of abuses, such as only a mob can invent.
3. And last they insult His divinity, thus virtually confessing their belief.

XXI.—THE FINAL JEWISH TRIAL

"And as soon as it was day, straightway all the chief priests and ancients of the people and scribes came together and held a council against Jesus to put Him to death. And they brought Him into their council, saying: If Thou be the Christ, tell us. And He said to them: If I shall tell you, you will not believe Me; and if I shall also ask you, you will not answer Me nor let Me go. But hereafter the Son of Man shall be sitting on the right hand of the power of God. Then said they all: Art Thou, then, the Son of God? And He said: You say that I am. Then they said: What need we any further testimony? For we ourselves have heard it from His own mouth. And the whole multitude of them rose up, and led Him away bound, and delivered Him to Pontius

Pilate the Governor."—Matt. xxvii. 1, 2; Mark xv. 1; Luke xxii. 66-71, xxiii. 1.

1. Our Lord's last night on earth is spent in prison. That fact has been the ground of endless meditation for all Christianity—above all, for those whose devotion clings about the Prisoner of Love in the Blessed Sacrament. What a lonely night! What a contrast to the quiet nights at Nazareth, or on the hillside with His Father, or even those nights in His preaching life when He had nowhere to lay His head, but depended on the charity of others! It is easier now to "watch one hour with Him" than in the Garden; now there is something that fascinates, and stirs compassion and love, in the lonely Prisoner.

2. And now the Jews can scarcely wait till daybreak; one wonders that they left Him at all. They assemble first among themselves to make sure of some safe course of action. Then comes the third trial. This time they will have no preliminaries. They have had enough of the false witnesses. They have found Him willing and foolish enough to play into their hands of His own accord. So they will begin there: "If Thou be the Christ, tell us." He had told them the night before. But this time He is not so easy to control. He begins with a rebuke, to which there is no answer but brute force; that rebuke which the persecutor must always meet with cruelty. "If I say 'yes,' I shall not be believed. If I prove, you will not meet My proofs.

Whatever I do or say, you will condemn Me." Then, again with that strength which dominates the whole story of the Passion, He speaks the plain truth; first enough to give them an escape if they will, but secondly, when they have explicitly rejected the grace, a clear statement of His divinity.

3. The condemnation follows. They do not pass the sentence in so many words; they are too cowardly for that. They just assume His guilt among themselves. "What need we more?" And before they have given themselves an answer they are already on their way through the streets. Is there anything more bitter to endure, by those who are in the right, than to be assumed guilty without trial? If on trial, to have all they say assumed to tell against them; whichever way they turn, to whatever they appeal, having all taken as proof of guilt, and all the time to be aware that the enemy more than suspects their innocence? Is not this the galling element of all persecution of the Church, particularly since the Reformation? Her error cannot be proved, because she is not in error; therefore either it must be assumed, or her truthful words must be so twisted till they become error.

Summary
1. The night with Our Lord in prison.
2. The last trial in the Jewish court.
3. The condemnation: "Not proven, but guilty."

XXII.—THE END OF JUDAS

"Then Judas, who betrayed Him, seeing that He was condemned, repenting himself, brought back the thirty pieces of silver to the chief priests and the ancients, saying: I have sinned in betraying innocent blood. But they said: What is that to us? look thou to it. And casting down the pieces of silver in the Temple, he departed and went and hanged himself with a halter. But the chief priests, having taken the pieces of silver, said: It is unlawful to put them into the corbona, because it is the price of blood. And having consulted together, they bought with them the potter's field, to be a burying-place for strangers. Wherefore that field was called Haceldama, that is, The field of blood, even to this day. Then was fulfilled that which was spoken by Jeremias the prophet, saying: And they took the thirty pieces of silver, the price of Him that was valued, whom they prized of the children of Israel. And they gave them unto the potter's field, as the Lord appointed to me."—Matt. xxvii. 3-10.

1. "Then Judas, who betrayed Him." The Evangelists cannot help repeating the description. It rankles in their hearts from first to last; it stings them to think that one of themselves should have brought all this about. "Repenting himself." A strange word here! Repenting, yet not repenting; for it was a repentance which led to greater misery. No man commits sin but he repents, in one sense; he will wish in some way that it were otherwise. But the repentance which makes us merely despise ourselves for cowards and worse is not

enough; there is repentance of this kind in despair.

2. "I have sinned." Judas confessed; so did the Prodigal, using the very same words; so did the penitent David; yet what a difference in the content of their words! Peter repented; yet with what a different result! Remorse is not contrition. Remorse follows on every sin so long as conscience is yet alive; it is Nature's guide to contrition; it may be made contrition by the life of love. But let alone it is merely self-disgust; it leads to despair, and despair leads to suicide, actual or virtual; how many souls have utterly destroyed themselves because they could no longer endure the sight of their own sinfulness! That remorse may become true sorrow it needs new life; new life can come only from love; of this Judas had none; the Prodigal, and David, and Magdalen, and Peter, had much; therefore much was forgiven them.

3. "What is that to us?" This is the other side of sin. Man sins against God, and appeals to God for mercy, and is forgiven; man sins to please the world, and appeals to the world for mercy, and is spurned aside. This is the very ugliest side of the world, its contempt for its own victims. It is nothing if not self-right-eous. It accepts another's service in evil; it flatters the man or woman that will ruin himself or herself to please it; it pays down its due, and thereby claims that it has fulfilled all justice.

But it contemns the slave who has served it; it washes its hands, its immaculate hands forsooth, of all responsibility; the soul that has submitted to be ruined must look to itself. "Am I my brother's keeper?" If my brother or my sister is willing to be ruined, is it not my brother's or my sister's fault, even if I am the cause of ruin? The quibbling, cruel world! Yet, poor world! it has enough of its own guilt to bear.

Summary

1. The meaning of barren repentance.
2. The meaning of true repentance.
3. Repentance and the two masters: God and the world.

XXIII.—THE FIRST CHARGE BEFORE PILATE

"Then they led Jesus from Caiphas to the Governor's hall. And it was morning, and they went not into the hall, that they might not be defiled, but that they might eat the Pasch. Pilate therefore went out to meet them, and said: What accusation bring you against this man? They answered and said to him: If He were not a malefactor, we would not have delivered Him up to thee."—John xviii. 28-30.

1. Here begins another of those dreadful processions, this time in broad daylight, right across the city, at an hour when the streets are busiest. A victim-priest of the revolution in Portugal once told me that of all the sufferings they had to undergo, and all were very terrible, none was so hard as the procession from time to time, to which they were sub-

mitted, through the streets of the city, with its hooting mob, made up of their own fellow-citizens, for whom they had given all their labor. At the gate of the Roman Governor's palace the procession stopped. The leaders would not enter. The formalities of their religion forbade it, and formalities were with them much more important than the Ten Commandments. So is the tendency in the East. So long as one observes the rites one is a good, religious man; sin is at worst only an uncleanness, which a rite at times can even sanction. But is this tendency only Eastern? Do we of the West never sacrifice truth for convention, for rite?

2. Pilate had to humor these Eastern fanatics. No doubt that was the policy of the Western government then, as it is more or less today. He must listen to them; as far as possible he must let them have their own way; it is enough if in the end the iron hand of law prevails. So, like a judge in a modern Eastern court, he asks them; not that he may hear the charge, but that he may discover what lies underneath. He knows they will not tell the truth; he knows the real motive will be hidden at first; they will begin with what they think will appeal to him as a Roman, as a judge, as a guardian of the peace; the rest will come later.

3. And he is not mistaken. "What accusation bring you against this man?" he asks. Their answer is obviously no answer. They dare not

yet say: "He declares Himself to be the Son of God." That would, as yet, mean nothing to Pilate. They dare not even accuse Him outright of being a malefactor; they know that an investigation, on strict Roman lines, would prove their charge untrue. So once more, as the cowardly world will always do, it formulates its charge as an asumption. "If He were not a malefactor, we would not have delivered Him up to thee." Here, then, is the first charge; how unlike anything we have yet heard! "Which of you shall accuse Me of sin?" He had once asked them; and they could answer nothing. "Because of Thy good works we blame Thee not," they had confessed another time. "He hath done all things well," had cried the people on another occasion. "If I have done evil, give testimony of the evil," He had said before Annas. And now, this!—"If He were not a malefactor!"

Summary

1. Watch the dragging of Our Lord through the city. Watch the formalism of the priests before Pilate.

2. Watch the attitude of Pilate, heartless, contemptuous, politic.

3. The first charge: Our Lord is assumed to be a malefactor.

XXIV.—THE SECOND CHARGE BEFORE PILATE

"Pilate then said to them: Take Him you, and judge Him according to your law. The Jews therefore said to him: It is not lawful for us to put anyone to death; that the word of Jesus might be fulfilled, signifying what death He should die. And they began to accuse Him, saying: We have found this man perverting our nation, and forbidding to give tribute to Caesar, and saying that He is Christ the King. And Jesus stood before Pilate the Governor. And Pilate asked Him, saying: Art Thou the King of the Jews? And Jesus answered him and said: Thou sayest it. And the chief priests and ancients accused Him in many things. And when He was accused He answered nothing."—Matt. xxvii. 11, 12; Mark xv. 2-5; Luke xxiii. 2, 3; John xviii. 31.

1. Pilate was not deceived; he knew that more would follow. If this was all, they need not have come to him; over mere malefactors their own court had jurisdiction. Again, if they had had any definite charge they would have made it; they would not have hidden themselves behind an assumption. So he forced them further. "If that is all," he said, "it comes into your court, not mine. So take Him you, and judge Him according to your law." His device succeeded. Judgment upon a malefactor was not what they wanted; they wanted blood, and before they had realized what they were saying they revealed their secret. "It is not lawful for us to put anyone to death." Now at least Pilate knew what was intended. It was a battle between

him and them for the life of Jesus Christ; it was he, not Our Lord, who was upon his trial.

2. The first shot had failed; that He was a malefactor was of no avail. They must try another; they will charge Him with high treason. And the charge has three degrees: First, "We have found this man perverting our nation"— He who had said: "I am come not to destroy, but to perfect." "Seek first the Kingdom of God and His justice, and all other things shall be added unto you." But this was of no avail; what was their "nation" to Pilate? Then came the second: "We have found this man forbidding to give tribute to Caesar"—He who, when these very Pharisees had tried to catch Him in His speech, had said: "Render unto Caesar the things that are Caesar's." This charge, too, Pilate could ignore; he knew well enough whether or not Rome was being cheated of her revenue; he knew, too, who were the men against whom that charge might have been more justly preferred.

3. Then came the final accusation: "We have found this man saying He is Christ the King." "Christ" meant nothing to Pilate, except that he may have known that the ancient Kings of Israel were "anointed." But "King" did mean something. It was a word both hateful and contemptible in the Republic of Rome. It was the mark, moreover, of a barbarian. But it was also a name to suspect. As Romans hated the

term, so barbarians revered it; and more than one revolt had been raised by some usurper simply taking on himself the title. About this, then, he would inquire. "Art Thou the King of the Jews?" he asked, partly in contempt, partly in curiosity, partly, perhaps, in suspicion. The answer is appallingly precise. Even Pilate himself must have been startled. "Thou sayest it. I am." Now, if Pilate pleased, he had technical ground to proceed against Our Lord; he had "heard it from His own mouth"; he needed no further evidence; yet his heart told him that for all that the man before him was not guilty.

Summary

1. The first charge of high treason.
2. The second charge of high treason.
3. The third charge of high treason.

XXV.—THE DEFENSE BEFORE PILATE

"Then Pilate again asked Him: Answerest Thou nothing? Behold in how many things they accuse Thee. Dost not Thou hear how great testimonies they allege against Thee? But Jesus still answered him not to any word, so that the Governor wondered exceedingly. Pilate therefore went into the hall again and called Jesus, and said to Him: Art Thou the King of the Jews? Jesus answered: Sayest thou this thing of thyself, or have others told it thee of Me? Pilate answered: Am I a Jew? Thy nation and the chief priests have delivered Thee up to me. What hast Thou done? Jesus answered: My kingdom is not of this world. If My kingdom were of this world, My servants would certainly strive that I should not be delivered to the Jews, but now My kingdom is not

*from hence. Pilate therefore said to him: Art thou
a King, then? Jesus answered: Thou sayest that I
am a King. For this was I born, and for this came
I into the world, that I should give testimony to the
truth. Everyone that is of the truth heareth My
voice. Pilate saith to Him: What is truth? And
when he had said this he went forth again to the
Jews, and saith to the chief priests and the multitude: I find no cause in this man."—Matt. xxvii. 13,
14; Mark xv. 4, 5; Luke xxiii. 4; John xviii. 33-38.*

1. In this conflict between the world and the
spirit we are struck first by the assumption of
authority in the one, and the reality of authority
in the other. Pilate is indeed on the chair of
justice, and Jesus is in the dock; but from first
to last it is easy to see which is master, which
acts upon the formality of power, and which
on the basis of true strength. The formality leads
to bullying, and bullying always betrays weakness, while strength can afford to be silent, and
silent strength is often the best proof of innocence. To such an argument Pilate was unac-
customed; it made him wonder; it made him
a little afraid; he felt he could not afford to
despise this man, however helpless and at his
mercy He appeared. So from that time to this
has the silence of Christ held the attention and
stirred the fear of the judging world.

2. Pilate would examine Him in private. On
only one point would he satisfy himself. He
knew He was not a malefactor; he made nothing
of the many other things that were alleged

against Him; but he must know about this title of King. He must not betray his own personal interest; he must not let it be supposed that he has any soul in the matter; he must pretend that it is merely a question of law that must be solved. Our Lord tries to get him to acknowledge the thing that is in his heart; He would have him own that he seeks, not as an empty judge, but as one who really "looked for the Kingdom of Israel," as other Romans had done who had already crossed His path. But Pilate "would not." He would be a man of the world to the end.

3. Still Jesus would fight for his soul. He would let Pilate see that he had nothing to fear from His Kingship and His Kingdom. He would thus lead him on to acknowledge the Kingdom that underlay all others, the truth which was the foundation of all kingdoms, of all society. He would bring home to him that it was possible to be a member of the Kingdom of Christ, and thereby all the better member of a kingdom of man. Pilate understood enough. He heard from Our Lord's own lips the confession that He was a King; but, unlike the scribes and ancients, he did not at once say: What need we any further testimony? He said: I find no cause in Him.

Summary

1. The silence of Our Lord is **and always has been** the answer to His calumniators.

2. The examination of Our Lord is a struggle to make Pilate true, not merely conventional.

3. It fails; but it wins a confession.

XXVI.—THE SUBJECT OF HEROD

"But they were more earnest, saying: He stirreth up the people, teaching throughout all Judaea, beginning from Galilee to this place. And Pilate, hearing Galilee, asked if the man were a Galilaean. And when he understood that He belonged to Herod's jurisdiction, he sent Him away to Herod, who himself was also at Jerusalem in those days."—Luke xxiii. 5-7.

1. The examination had been in private; the priests therefore did not know what had passed between the judge and their Victim. But something assured them that the charge of high treason had gone home. They must cling to that. So they fall back upon it, this time coloring the truth so that it seems the blackest lie. For, indeed, what they now have to say is only the simple truth; He had stirred up the people, He had taught throughout all Judea, He had begun from as far as Galilee and had reached even up to that place. Everywhere he had proclaimed His Kingdom, saying: "Do penance, for the Kingdom of Heaven is at hand." He had so won the hearts of men that these scribes and Pharisees and priests and ancients had met together in dismay, saying: "What do we? for behold the world goes after Him?" He had gone about doing good; the good He had done had been acknowledged even by His enemies.

and now because He had done it, because He had given Himself unsparingly for God and man, therefore, with the cleverness of Satan, it could be shown that He was a danger to the State. And the argument still holds.

2. "Pilate, hearing Galilee, asked if the man were a Galilaean." This would seem to show conclusively that Pilate had heard little or nothing of Our Lord before. Though "all the world" had been going after Him; though there had been the great display of palms on the Sunday before; though in the booths and the market-place the question whether Jesus of Nazareth were or were not in the city was on the lips of many; still, the great ones in the land knew nothing of Him, and those who guided the destinies of nations had never heard of the man that was revolutionizing the world. "Jesus of Nazareth passes by"; and only the blind see Him, and the lame follow Him, and the deaf hear Him, and the weak things of this world are chosen to confound the strong; but the great and the strong do not know Him, never hear of Him, or if they do only know Him as one who "stirreth up the people" and must be suppressed.

3. "He sent Him away to Herod." Here begins Our Lord's third procession through the city; we cannot recall these processions without reminding ourselves of their peculiar sufferings, the special insults to which they exposed Him

"in the house of them that loved Him"—insults which, in the crowded interest of the rest, are too easily overlooked. On Pilate's part it was an act of cowardice, a deliberate shirking of responsibility; since he could not bring himself as yet to put an innocent man to death to please the mob, he hoped the less scrupulous Herod would do it for him. He had played with the situation from the beginning; now his playing was bringing its results—growing guilt upon himself; increasing suffering for Our Lord.

Summary

1. The new charge, found in the truth, the wells having been poisoned.

2. The ignorance of Our Lord shown by Pilate, in spite of many circumstances.

3. Pilate's cowardice before temptation, increasing his own guilt and the suffering of Our Lord.

XXVII.—JESUS BEFORE HEROD

"And Herod, seeing Jesus, was very glad, for he was desirous of a long time to see Him, because he had heard many things of Him, and he hoped to see some miracle wrought by Him. And he questioned Him with many words. But He answered him nothing. And the chief priests and scribes stood by, earnestly accusing Him. And Herod with his soldiers despised Him, and mocked Him, putting on Him a white garment, and sent Him back to Pilate. And Herod and Pilate were made friends together that same day, for before they were enemies one to another."—Luke xxiii. 8-12.

1. Our Lord will have it so arranged that the three great sources of evil in this world shall

be brought face to face with Him in this hour of darkness; and Herod is particularly easy to distinguish. He is the man who represented the loathsome resultant of Eastern and Western luxury combined; the man who belonged to no creed, to no nationality, to no moral standard; the man who had defied all decency in his marriage, who had murdered John the Baptist to please a dancing girl, and that in the midst of revelry; the man who had one besetting misery, the fear of his victim rising up against him; the man who alone of all mankind had won from Our Lord a term of indignant contempt. "Go and tell that fox!" Jesus had said of him on one occasion. Thus he stands, the judge of Jesus Christ, this personification of that selfish luxury and indulgence which stalks through the world, defying God and man, but despised by man and God, the source of misery upon misery.

2. The trial befits the judge. His one aim in life is self-indulgence; even a criminal must serve for his amusement. And this Criminal is one who will excellently serve his turn. He is said to work miracles; He is the most expert conjuror of the day. He is said to be a prophet; He is the best inventor of witticisms. He shall give proof of His skill, for Herod's amusement and for the amusement of his court; otherwise He shall pay for it. Meanwhile, the light and easy way in which he treats the whole affair

makes "the chief priests and scribes" anxious.
The judge does not appear to be in earnest;
perhaps in the end he will dismiss the whole
affair and let Jesus go. Perhaps Jesus Himself
will work some miracle and win His liberty. So
they renew their accusations; they clamor all
around against Him. "The chief priests and
scribes stood by, earnestly accusing Him."

3. But Herod is disappointed; the Criminal
ignores him. Our Lord had before him a "fox,"
a contemptible creature; He now treats him as
such. The tables are being turned. Herod had
thought to make Our Lord appear as a fool
before his court; and behold, it is he that is
being made to look foolish. This must be stopped.
Since Jesus will not play His part of a fool,
He shall be made one. Since He will obviously
win if fairly treated, He shall be conquered
by laughter and mockery and derision, the fav-
orite resort of the luxurious, self-indulgent
world. So the mockery begins; Herod begins
it, demeaning himself that he may demean Our
Lord; the soldiers follow the example of their
master, and Our Lord stands there, in His
white fool's robe, the despised of men, the outcast of the people, a new torture in the story
of the Passion.

Summary

1. Herod, the representative of the cowardly indulgence of men.

2. His trial of Our Lord turned into a scene of merciless revelry.

3. To save himself from disgrace, Herod dressed Our Lord as a fool.

XXVIII.—THE FIRST SENTENCE OF PILATE

"Then Pilate, calling together the chief priests and the magistrates and the people, said to them: You have brought this man to me as one that perverteth the people; and behold I, having examined Him before you, find no cause in this man touching those things wherein you accuse Him. No, nor yet Herod, for I sent you to him, and behold, nothing worthy of death is done to Him. I will chastise Him, therefore, and release Him."—Luke xxiii. 14-16.

1. This scene closes another chapter in the story of the Passion. We know the last step in serious temptation. We would have the gratification, but we would not have the responsibility which it entails. We protest we do not want the sin; we only want the satisfaction; and we try to persuade ourselves in consequence that we shall not be guilty. So here. The Jews have shirked the responsibility of murdering Our Lord; Herod has shirked it; now Pilate makes a last attempt to do the same before the final plunge. Later, it is true, he makes other attempts; but here he accepts the responsibility of the last word. Therefore, he makes it as formal as possible; as throughout the rest of the Passion, he seems to say, "If I am guilty, others shall be guilty with me"; and it is only

at the end, when the Jews have agreed to share the full responsibility with himself, that he finally gives way. This, again, is another of the characteristics of grievous sin; it seems to find some covering for its malice in making and finding others as bad as itself.

2. But the worst of all is the sentence: "Therefore." Because the two chief courts in Jerusalem have found this man not guilty, therefore I will chastise Him. Because He is evidently something above us all, commanding us all even as He stands in bonds, therefore I will chastise Him. Because He has spoken to me of the truth, has roused in me deeper thoughts, deeper reverence, than anyone has ever roused before, therefore I will chastise Him. Because, if I would allow Him, He would teach me things that would alter all my life, therefore I will chastise Him. Because these people envy Him—in other words, acknowledge by their hate that He is something better than themselves—therefore I will chastise Him. And then I will let Him go. I will still pose as His deliverer. He shall still have to say that He owes His life to me. To chastise Him is the less of two evils. How often has the same sentence been passed upon Him and His own! "He is not guilty; others envy Him; I will chastise Him therefore; I will reduce Him; and then I will let Him go."

3. The picture is pitiable; there are few sights more pitiable than a judge that is unjust through

94

cowardice. Here judges play the weakling; the clamoring mob is at the mercy of its own contemptible passions; Herod, a disappointed and secretly embittered creature; the Victim alone the Master of them all. One feels through it all how Gethsemani is having its effect, and that He has indeed been strengthened. He is no longer, as before the prayer in the Garden, "sorrowful even unto death," a broken man, frightened and beside Himself with fear. Had He so willed it, He might have gone through the Passion in the same broken way; He might have gone on crying: "Take this chalice from Me." But no; His prayer has been heard, and the strength to endure never leaves Him.

Summary

1. The first sentence of Pilate is an attempt to distinguish between sin and its guilt.
2. The cruelty of the sentence is manifest; yet how often repeated!
3. In the whole scene, how mean do all the actors appear except One.

XXIX.—JESUS OR BARABBAS?

"Now upon the solemn festival day the Governor was accustomed to release to the people one of the prisoners, whosoever they demanded. And he had then a notorious prisoner that was called Barabbas, a robber who was put in prison with seditious men, who in the sedition had committed murder. And when the multitude was come up, they began to desire what he always had done to them. And Pilate answered them and said: You have a custom that

THE CROWN OF SORROW

I should release one unto you at the Pasch. Wi
you, therefore, that I release unto you the King o
the Jews? Whom will you that I release to you
Barabbas, or Jesus who is called Christ? For h
knew that through envy the chief priests had de
livered Him up."—Matt. xxvii. 15-18; Mark xv. 6-10
Luke xxiii. 17; John xviii. 39, 40.

1. We do not know much of this annual custon
of the Roman power in Jerusalem. No doubt i
was one of those formalities of clemency b
which an alien conqueror tries to humor an
reconcile the conquered. Hence, no doubt, i
would have been mainly political prisoners tha
would have been released; the release of thieve
and cut-throats could have had no meaning. Ou
Lord, as "King," as "the Christ," as a "seduce
of the people," as one who "forbade to giv
tribute to Caesar," was mainly a political pris
oner; the charge of being a "malefactor" ha
long since died away. Barabbas, on the othe
hand, though a political prisoner, was primaril
a malefactor; he had made use of a seditio
not so much for purposes of State, as for rob
bery and murder. The contrast was marked
Pilate emphasized it; he hoped by making a
impossible offer to compel the people to acquiesc

2. But the people were at bay. Under othe
circumstances they could never have wished fo
Barabbas; thieves and cut-throats could hav
won no favor from them. Still, though the
did not want Barabbas, they wanted Our Lo
still less; their hatred of Him made their hatre

of Barabbas appear almost like affection; at all events it should appear like affection in order the more to justify themselves in their own eyes. So had it been between Pilate and Herod; their scorn of Our Lord had softened their scorn for each other into friendship, And so it is today; the "sign which shall be contradicted" has drawn together in alliance causes and powers the most irreconcilable. They do not hate each other less, but they hate Him more; and that becomes their bond of sympathy and union.

3. It remains to study the words of Pilate. He knew that envy was at the bottom of the charge; and the envy was mainly confined to "the chief priests." Envy of what? "He stirreth up the people." "Behold, all the world goes after Him." "They dared not lay hands on Him for fear of the people." "It is expedient that one man should die for the people." Therefore to the people, over the heads of the chief priests and leaders, Pilate would appeal. The people had before wished to make Him King; would they now desert Him? They had hailed Him as "He that cometh in the name of the Lord"; would they now surrender, in place of Barabbas, Jesus Who is called the Christ"? There was reason to hope that they would be shamed into releasing one Whom they had recently acclaimed, One Who, above all, had such influence upon them.

Summary

1. Jesus, political prisoner and "malefactor" Barabbas, malefactor and political prisoner.
2. The hatred of Jesus the bond of union.
3. Pilate appeals to the people over the heads of the priests.

XXX.—THE REJECTION

"But the chief priests and ancients persuaded the people that they should ask Barabbas and make Jesus away. And the Governor, answering, said to them: Which will you have of the two to be released unto you? But the whole multitude cried out at once saying: Away with this man and release unto us Barabbas. And Pilate spoke to them again, desiring to release Jesus: What will you then that I do with Jesus, that is called Christ, the King of the Jews? But they all again cried out: Crucify Him, crucify Him, let Him be crucified! And Pilate said to them the third time: Why, what evil hath He done? I find no cause of death in Him. I chastise Him, therefore, and let Him go. But they were the more instant with loud voices: Crucify Him, let Him be crucified! and their voices prevailed."—Matt. xxvii. 20-24; Mark xv. 11-15; Luke xxiii. 18-23.

1. There is hope in the thought that if left to themselves the multitude might have been won over by Pilate. Seldom, if ever, is it that the multitude is wholly to blame for its misdeeds. The multitude is usually irresponsible; it is the leaders that are to blame—a principle of history which historians often ignore to suit their purpose. Here we can follow the influence at work, the persuasion of the Governor; the meek yet

98

commanding figure of Our Lord; the acknowl-
edgement, if they would listen to it, that they
had suffered only kindness at His hands. But
on the other hand was the awe of the chief
priests and ancients; the blind excitement about
they knew not what; the knowledge that to
accept this Christ was to accept a new standard,
such as condemned their present life.

2. So they made their choice, recklessly,
sweepingly, with their eyes closed to all consequences, as a man will do whose passion governs
him, who has at last become the victim of a
temptation, who will see but one object to be
gained, the immediate satisfaction of his desire,
come what else may hereafter. But the course
along which passion leads is hard to alter; the
leap leads to a headlong fall beyond; reason
is ignored, restraint is resented, each step made
does but compel one to more and more daring.
So it is with the Jews. Christ is a malefactor.
No; He is not. Christ is a traitor. He is not
that either. Christ is a sham and a mounte-
bank. He is not guilty. "Very well, whatever
He is, malefactor or not, traitor or not, mounte-
bank or not, still 'Away with Him! Crucify
Him let Him be crucified!' even if it be for
no reason whatsoever but because we wish it."

3. Pilate pleaded; let us give him this credit.
Let us recognize his sincerity in that at least
he wished to save Our Lord. Later Our Lord
Himself virtually told him that he was the least

99

guilty of the chief actors in the crime. He had but human standards, the standards of circumstance, and opportunity,, and convention; he had no God in his horizon, "truth" to him meant nothing; in all this he was no worse and no better than the world in which he lived, or than the world in which we live ourselves. He, too, would see no flaw in the saying of Caiphas: "It is expedient that one man should die for the people." Left alone, he might have done no harm to anyone. He was one to whom his religious-minded wife could give a warning. But in a moment such as this, as is invariably the case when the standard of the world is tested, he broke down.

Summary

1. The multitude, itself, perhaps, inclined to good, is beaten by its leaders.

2. Hence the choice, reckless of consequences.

3. Pilate, the type of this world's judgment, is also inclined to good, but is beaten.

XXXI.—THE CONDEMNATION

"And Pilate, seeing that he prevailed nothing, but rather that a tumult was made, having taken water, washed his hands before the people, saying: I am innocent of the blood of this just man; look you to it. And all the people answering said: His blood be upon us and upon our children. Then Pilate, being willing to satisfy the people, gave sentence that their petition should be granted. And he released unto them Barabbas, who for murder and sedition had been cast into prison, whom they had desired, but delivered up to them Jesus, when he had scourged

THE CONDEMNATION

Him, to be crucified according to their will."—Matt. xxvii. 24-26; Mark xv. 15; Luke xxiii. 23-25; John xix. 13-16.

1. It is in this scene that Pilate displays his greatest meanness, which is common. The priests and ancients showed it when, having induced Judas to sin, they turned on him and said: "What is that to us? Look you to it." Cain showed it when, after the murder of his brother, he said: "Am I my brother's keeper?" Of all the meanness of this mean world, nothing is so mean, yet scarcely anything is so common, as to induce another into sin, or to sin along with another, and then to decline the responsibility of the crime; to murder another's soul, another's honor, and then to say: "I am innocent of the blood of this man. He could have helped Himself if He had chosen. I am in a difficult position. If there is guilt at all, it is not mine who do the deed, but His who permits me to do it, or those who make me do it. I am innocent, though the deed is mine."

2. And yet one is appalled at the opposite extreme. If it is mean to put on other shoulders the guilt of sin of which we have in any way been the cause, it is even more terrible so to contemn the guilt of sin as to accept it for oneself with both hands. There are those who know no better, to whom sin has no more meaning than an illicit prank, though these are fewer than at first it might seem. There are those

101

who look on sin as a matter of this life alone, an offense against man, against the law, against their own common sense and conscience. Of these one need not here think. And there are those who, with eyes wide open, knowing both the meaning and the guilt of sin, yet in their passion will accept the full burden, the burden which broke Our Lord Himself in the Garden. "His blood be upon us and upon our children" is an act of more determined suicide than that of Judas; and yet in every great sin that is determinedly committed one hears the echo of the same words.

3. There follows the condemnation and the preliminary scourging; it is a fitting scene after this terrible manifestation of weakness on one side and malice on the other. "I will chastise Him, therefore, and let Him go," has now been changed into, "I will chastise Him, therefore, and then will crucify Him." The worldling has been beaten; his support has only added to the agony of the Passion; at the last moment he has betrayed his imagined Protégé; and he has done it with a show of dignity and injured innocence which, he hopes, may secure his good name and good estate. But Our Lord is scourged; Our Lord is stripped naked, and tied to a pillar, and scourged; in the presence of anyone who cares to come and see, He is treated as a felon and scourged. We can come; we can see; but how long can we dare to look?

Summary

1. Pilate, the type of that mean worldling who would sin but lay on others the guilt.

2. The crowd, the type of that other extreme which would defy guilt.

3. For all this Our Lord is scourged.

XXXII.—THE CROWNING WITH THORNS

"Then the soldiers of the Governor, taking Jesus into the court of the palace, gathered together unto Him the whole band, and stripping Him, they put a scarlet cloak about Him. And platting a crown of thorns, they put it upon His head, and a reed in His right hand. And they came to Him, and bowing the knee before Him, they mocked Him, and began to salute Him, saying: Hail, King of the Jews! And they gave Him blows, and they did spit upon Him, and they took the reed and struck His head, and bowing their knees, they worshipped Him."—Matt. xxvii. 27-29; Mark xv. 16-19; John xix. 14, 15.

1. When Our Lord prophesied His Passion to His disciples on His last journey to Jerusalem, He seemed to linger upon the scene here described, as though it had for Him a sense of special horror. "Behold we go up to Jerusalem," He said, "and the Son of Man shall be betrayed to the chief priests, and to the scribes and ancients, and they shall condemn Him to death, and shall deliver Him to the Gentiles. And they shall mock Him, and spit upon Him, and scourge Him, and kill Him; and the third day He shall rise again." Throughout meditation on the Passion there is little need to look for application;

its own dead weight should be enough, pressing down on us as it pressed down on Him; in scenes such as this, in particular, we need do no more than try to realize what they contained. To do so is to grow in sympathy, and sympathy is love.

2. The chief actors in this scene were Roman soldiers, men of blood, of no principle, fostered in brutality. They gathered in their numbers, thus encouraging each other, rivaling each other, in ingenious cruelty. They had been trained in contempt for the title of King; how much more must they contemn one whose claim had stripped Him; the shame of it!—they clad Him in the mock robe of a King!—they seated Him upon a mock throne!—they made a mock crown, of the thorny brambles used for the fire, and hammered down upon His head!—they took a reed from the rushes lying on the floor, and put it in His hand, and behold He was crowned a fool king! We can hear the ribald laughter. We can see the writhing form, helplessly rolling beneath the pressure of the thorns. We can ask ourselves what it means, and be aghast at the thought that love is its only explanation.

3. After the crowning must come the doing of homage. They came to Him in a mock procession. They strutted up to Him, they bowed down before Him, they genuflected. They saluted Him, and said: "Hail, King of the Jews!" in a mock solemn voice. And then, as each rose in

"To Thee, O Jesus, I recommend my parents, relatives and friends, and all the living and dead who by their prayers and sacrifices have helped me to Thy Holy Altar."

✝

Rev. Amos F. Gaudette
S. S. J.

Ordained Priest
May 28, 1942

First Solemn Mass.
May 31, 1942

✝

To Thee Jesus through Mary By the Grace of God I am what I am A Priest forever.

—1 Cor. XV: 10

QUEEN OF MOTHERS

turn from his act of obeisance, when it was the custom for a courtier to make his offering, even as at Bethlehem the Magi laid out their gifts before Him, then was the moment for individual ingenuity. As they rose up, one would strike Him in the face; another would spit upon Him; another would hammer down the crown more tightly; another would snatch the reed from His feeble hand, and would smite Him with it; another would prefer his foot, or the flat of his hand, perhaps fling at Him the filth on the floor. So do they worship Him: and we?

Summary

1. This is a scene which Our Lord particularly felt; we should find it easy to compassionate.

2. First is the mock crowning of the King, by such men, in such a manner.

3. Then is the mock homage paid to Him, with all its cruel devices.

XXXIII.—"ECCE HOMO"

"Pilate therefore went forth again, and saith to them: Behold I bring Him forth to you, that you may know that I find no cause in Him. (So Jesus came forth, bearing the crown of thorns, and the purple garment.) And he saith to them: Behold the man! When the chief priests, therefore, and the officers had seen Him, they cried out, saying: Crucify Him, crucify Him! Pilate saith to them: Take Him you, and crucify Him, for I find no cause in Him. The Jews answered him: We have a law, and according to that law He ought to die, because He made Himself the Son of God."—John xix. 4-7.

105

1. Pilate, by making this public show of Our Lord crowned with thorns, sanctioned the cruelty of the soldiers. If they had not done it at his order, at least by this he gave it his approval. Indeed, he must have known all the time what was being done, since he chose this particular moment, and this particular condition of the Victim, for the demonstration. And he gives his reason for his connivance; in his own mind he is cruel that he may be kind. By reducing Our Lord to this pitiable condition, he hopes to win the pity even of His enemies. Hence we may conclude that never in all the Passion does Our Lord appear more pitiable, more "a worm and no man, and the outcast of the people," than when He drags Himself up those steps, bent with exhaustion and agony, a mangled remnant of a body, clad in nothing but a scarlet rag with a helmet of thorns upon His head, to be shown as a spectacle to His own people.

2. *"Ecce homo"*—"Behold the man!" For indeed it needs to be labelled as a human being, this grovelling creature, this "worm and no man," whose humanity seems to have been beaten out of Him, and to have left nothing but a heap of blood and flesh. "From the crown of His head to the sole of His foot there is no soundness in Him"; this is literally true. And on the other hand, while He is a man and not a lower creature, who will say now that He is God? He is man, "the most abject of men," and no

one, pagan or Jew, can reconcile this with their idea of God. Surely then, now, if only out of pity and contempt, they will let Him go. So might well argue the pagan Pilate, and comfort his conscience that this act of flagrant injustice was after all most just—that line of argument which the merciless, temporizing world is for ever using to itself.

3. But not so the Jewish chief priests. It was not that they were by nature more cruel than Pilate! paganism is always by nature cruel; it was that religious cruelty—*corruptio optimi pessima*— can outstrip any cruelty that is in human nature. And the reason for their cruelty is at last made manifest. We have had it expressed in the courts of Annas and Caiphas; we have heard it in the course of our Lord's life; but so far it has not been uttered before Pilate. Now, in the paroxysm of their rage, the truth appears. "We want His life, not because He is a malefactor, not because He perverteth our nation, not because He forbiddeth to give tribute to Caesar, not because He sayeth He is Christ the King, but because He made Himself the Son of God. We want His life because this declaration goes against us and our ideas. Such a Son of God is not the Son of God for whom we look. Therefore, let Him be crucified."

Summary

1. The scene of the "Ecce homo" wins our pity and compassion, perhaps more than any other.

2. He is "a worm and no man," in the mind of the pagan proved not to be divine.

3. But in the mind of the Jew this very sight might prove His Godhead; therefore He must die.

XXXIV.—THE LAST INTERVIEW WITH PILATE

"When Pilate therefore had heard this saying, he feared the more. And he entered into the hall again, and he said to Jesus: Whence art Thou? But Jesus gave him no answer. Pilate therefore saith to Him: Speakest Thou not to me? Knowest Thou not that I have power to crucify Thee, and I have power to release Thee? Jesus answered: Thou shouldst not have any power against Me, unless it were given thee from above. Therefore he that hath delivered Me to thee hath the greater sin."—John xix. 8-11.

1. Our Lord once said: "He that is not with Me is against Me." But there are those who seem to be neither for Him nor against Him; who favor Him, but will not be allied with Him; who encourage Him, but will not help Him; who are friends with Him, but will not confess Him, who acknowledge His good works, but yet do not and will not know Him; who admire Him as a man, but as God have no interest in Him; if they have heard of Him as the Son of God, it has only made them restless, then curious, then assertive of their own authority lest they be conquered by Him; finally, because He has proved harmless to them, they have in some way shown themselves favorable to Him. Such, for the most part, is the non-religious world—above all, the non-religious

ruling world. It inquires, it threatens, but always assumes that it, and it alone, has "power to crucify, and power to release."

2. There is another element in the world of men, which, as Our Lord here says, "hath the greater sin." It is that which consists of those on whom religion has set its mark. To have known Him and to have rejected Him; to have condemned Him because He has "made Himself the Son of God"; to have stirred up the non-religious world against Him on this account; to have done Him to death, ignoring His claim, ignoring His good works, ignoring His singular and thrice-proved innocence; to have so confused the issue that the Son of God should be done to death as a political danger: those who have done this have "the greater sin." The powers that rule the world have the standards of the world, and these powers they have from God, though they know Him not; but they pretend to no more than the things of this world, until another power compels them to take cognizance of the things of God. Then perforce they must judge God by their own standards, for which He is too great. Then they find thmselves not with Him, but against Him.

3. But the three forces are at work in each one of us. One part is with Our Lord; another is not with Him, but neither would it be against Him; and this, in most of us, is the power that is strongest. Then there is the third, the power

within us which would have its own complete way, which would make its own faith and its own morals, which knows from afar that the teaching of the Son of God is for it "a hard saying," which cannot hope to serve two masters. This sets itself against the Son of God; it lays at His door all manner of charges, finding their justification in His mutilated words or His interpreted actions. It denounces Him to the neutral element within us, not at first on the ground that He is our enemy, but that He is the enemy of human freedom. Hence the battle in each soul and for each soul.

Summary

1. Pilate represents here the "neutral" world.
2. The Jews represent the avowed enemies of faith.
3. In each one's soul Christ, Pilate, and the Jews have their counterparts.

XXXV.—THE LAST DEFEAT OF PILATE

"And from thenceforth Pilate sought to release Him. But the Jews cried out, saying: If thou release this man, thou art not Caesar's friend, for whosoever maketh himself a King speaketh against Caesar. Now when Pilate had heard these words, he brought Jesus forth, and sat down in the judgment-seat, in the place that is called Lithostrotos, and in Hebrew, Gabbatha. And it was the Parasceve of the Pasch, about the sixth hour, and he saith to the Jews: Behold your King! But they cried out: Away with Him, away with Him, crucify Him! Pilate saith to them: Shall I crucify your King? The chief priests answered: We have no King but Caesar. Then there-

fore he delivered Him to them to be crucified."—
John xix. 12-16.

1. From thenceforth Pilate sought to release Him." The sentence seems out of place.
Had not Pilate been seeking to release Him from
the very outset? He had twice said that he
would do so. Yet St. John clearly means something very particular by this renewed statement.
Evidently this new charge, of "making Himself
the Son of God," and the dignity with which
Our Lord had received it, had had a deep effect.
There was something more than human in one
Who through all this could remain so calm and
commanding, Who could with such firmness act
as the Judge of His judges, and yet would not
move a finger in His own defense. Everything
had gone in Our Lord's favor; this last charge
of all, that He was the Son of God, was con-
firmed by all that had gone before. Pilate would
save Him if he could.

2. Now was the critical moment; the Jews
must play their last card, must surrender their
all to gain their point. For a moment it looked
as if at this last moment they were about to
be baffled. But Pilate, like every Roman, like
every Englishman, like every man who is proud
of an ideal, had the weakness of his strength.
Whatever else he was, he was a Roman; attack
him there, and there was no knowing what he
might not be induced to do. He did not realize
that to be a true Roman it was first necessary

to be a true man. "Thou art not Caesar's friend." This was a revelation. He had been shielding a "King"; might this be construed as un-Roman? Jesus was innocent; He was a doer of good; He was there "out of envy"; but He had some kind of title, which He claimed; was not that enough? Whatever else Pilate was, no slur must be cast upon his Roman honor.

3. The ruse succeeded; but at what a cost! "The chief priests answered: We have no King but Caesar!" Speaking for their whole people, in the presence of Jews, Gentiles, and Our Lord Himself, these chief priests made a formal renunciation of their inheritance. It was not merely that they rejected Our Lord; they no longer said they would not have Him to reign over them; their renunciation is more sweeping: "We have no King but Caesar." They renounce their independence as a nation; they tear up the promise of God, cherished through the centuries, of the King to Whom was promised the throne of David His father; they were no longer the chosen people of God; they would sacrifice their birthright that they might compass their design; the Kingdom was taken from them, as Our Lord had foretold, and given to a nation yielding the fruits thereof.

Summary

1. Pilate sought more than ever to release the "Son of God."

2. But the argument of disloyalty to his superior beat him.

3. And the Jews, accepting Caesar, renounced for ever their own inheritance.

XXXVI.—SIMON OF CYRENE

"And after they had mocked Him, they took off the purple cloak from Him, and put on Him His own garments, and led Him away to crucify Him. And as they led Him away, they found a man of Cyrene, named Simon, who passed by coming out of the country, the father of Alexander and of Rufus; him they forced to take up His cross to carry after Jesus."—Matt. xxvii. 31, 32; Mark xv. 20. 21; Luke xxiii. 26; John xix. 16.

1. Catholic devotion lingers over this last journey of Our Lord from the hall of Pilate to the hill of Calvary, and one may well in meditation follow Him step by step as far as one is able. The Evangelists tell the story of this journey in the fewest words, as if they were anxious to hurry over it; no doubt the journey itself was a hurried thing, the enemies of Our Lord being only too eager, now that the doom had been definitely secured, to have everything over and done with as soon as possible. There must be no delay, no hindrance; Pilate might again change his mind at the last moment; and besides, the Paschal hour was coming on. The distance from the hall to the hill was but half a mile; but the streets were crowded, there were many turnings and corners, there was some confusion in the making of the procession with its combined Jews and Romans and

its three victims, and, above all, the exhausted state of Our Lord Jesus Christ Himself made them wonder whether He would reach the place of execution alive.

2. So the hurried march began. Tradition has filled up many gaps, and we may well include them here. They restored to Him His clothes, not so much out of humanity, but that He might be the more easily recognized on the road, and because the clothing of an executed man was the perquisite of the executioners. He received His cross; there was joy mixed with sorrow in the gift. From this solemn moment, with this weapon He was to conquer; this was to be His standard, for each and all of His followers to embrace. He went a little further; He stumbled and fell; for there in front of Him was something which had caught His eye, and had shaken Him with emotion. It was His Mother, standing with a few companions at a corner of the street. Where had she been all this time? Saints tell us many details. They saw one another; probably there was no word; but we can well imagine her "Behold the handmaid of the Lord" struggling with her "Son, why hast Thou done so to us?" as she watches her Child pass by.

3. Then the strength of Our Lord begins to give out. He must be assisted, or He will die on the way. A laboring man of Cyrene meets the procession. He has no interest in this busi-

114

ness; it is to him only one more outbreak of
a cruel Eastern mob, and he would gladly pass
it by. But he is stopped, and "forced to take
up His cross to carry after Jesus." He is an-
noyed; he is ashamed; he is insulted; he resents
being made the servant of a criminal. Yet we
are sure that before he had laid that cross
down he had become a follower of Our Lord
in a fuller sense; for the Evangelists linger with
love over his name, and over the names of his
two sons, telling us without any doubt that
they are among their friends to whom the whole
Church would be eternally indebted. We live
our day; we do little things and great; one
day we walk down a street, and a sufferer meets
us, and a cross is flung on our shoulders, and
we resent it, and that is the moment of our
lives.

Summary

1. The scene of the Way of the Cross, and the
circumstances, should be taken in detail.

2. The first stations: the receiving of the cross,
the first fall, the meeting with the Mother.

3. Simon of Cyrene is forced to take up the cross
to carry after Jesus.

XXXVII.—THE WOMEN OF JERUSALEM

*"And there followed Him a great multitude of
people and of women, who bewailed and lamented
Him. But Jesus, turning to them, said: Daughters
of Jerusalem, weep not over Me, but weep for yourselves and for your children. For, behold, the day
shall come wherein they will say: Blessed are the*

barren, and the wombs that have not borne, and the breasts that have not given suck. Then shall they begin to say to the mountains: Fall upon us, and to the hills, Cover us. For if in the green wood they do these things, what shall be done in the dry?"— Luke xxiii. 27-31.

1. This little scene, told appropriately by St. Luke, the Evangelist of sympathy and the friend of women, comes as a great relief in the long tale of agony. Hitherto one might have been led to suppose that all Jerusalem was against Our Lord. Now we discover in the crowd some at least who sympathize; and these are not a few, for St. Luke describes them as "a great multitude of people and of women." The scene, therefore, as usually described and pictured is misleading. Not only women bewailed Him, but a great multitude besides; these were not met along the roadside by accident, but they "followed Him"; they did not merely weep at the sudden sight of so much suffering, but they "bewailed and lamented" Him continuously. It is a joy to us to know that these were there; we would give much to know the name of even one in that "multitude." There is something that tells us that compassion such as this must find its reward in Heaven.

2. To this multitude only, and directly only to the women in this multitude, does Our Lord appear to have spoken all the way from the Praetorium to Calvary. And His words are as mysterious as their setting; they recall the

thunder-clouds that hang over the prophets of
old, they almost repeat the warnings of His own
last days in the Temple. They are not to weep
over Him; but that, we may justly suppose He
did not mean literally. He "looked for one that
would weep together with Him, and there was
none"; in the words of another prophecy, He
appealed: "All you that pass by the way, attend
and see if there be sorrow like to My sorrow."
All His life He had shown that He was hurt
when He was cut; that He was full of gratitude
to anyone who showed Him the least interest or
sympathy. And now the very fact that He spoke
to this group shows that He felt their regard,
even as later He felt the companionship of the
penitent thief, and of Mary and John.

3. But like those whose power of sympathy
is very great, for the moment the future sufferings of others overcame His own. His compassion was greater than His Passion; He suffered
in others even more than He suffered in Himself.
He recalled to them the prophecy of Osee:
"Samaria hath made her King to pass as froth
upon the face of the water. And the high places
of the idol, the sin of Israel shall be destroyed:
the burr and the thistle shall grow up over the
altars: and they shall say to the mountains:
Cover us; and to the hills: Fall upon us." The
doom was on the city because it had not known
the day of its visitation; this even now Our
Lord cannot put away from His mind. "For if

117

in the green wood they do these things, what shall be done in the dry?" Who do the words mean? Does St. Peter paraphrase them when he says: "If the just man shall scarcely be saved, where shall the ungodly and the sinner appear?"

Summary

1. "A great multitude of people and of women" sympathized with Our Lord.
2. Our Lord cherished that sympathy.
3. But His own power of sympathy made Him feel for them even more.

XXXVIII.—THE CRUCIFIXION

"And bearing His own Cross, He went forth to that place which is called Calvary, but in Hebrew Golgotha. And they gave Him to drink wine mingled with myrrh. And when He had tasted, He would not drink. And there were also two other malefactors, led with Him to be put to death. And when they were come to the place they crucified Him there; and the robbers, one on the right hand, and the other on the left. And the Scripture was fulfilled which saith: And with the wicked He was reputed."—Matt. xxvii. 33, 34; Mark xv. 22, 23; Luke xxiii. 32, 33; John xix. 17, 18.

1. This crowning act of the Passion, the Crucifixion, is told in a cold, matter-of-fact way by all the Evangelists. The details are the same in each case; including every variation and addition, we have but a few lines. The exact spot we know. Scholars may dispute about other sites, the Cave of Bethlehem, the House of

Nazareth, the place of the Last Supper, but of Calvary there is no reasonable doubt. The Evangelists themselves are careful to note the spot; they take the same care over no other, giving the name in two languages, etc. No wonder; for it is the most sacred spot upon this earth— the one spot which has been steeped in the Blood of Our Saviour Jesus Christ, the one source from which has sprung the stream that has regenerated the world.

2. The details of the Crucifixion are few. The executioners had still in them a touch of legalized humanity. They offered Our Lord the partly stupefying drink which was offered to all condemned criminals before the butchery began. We could have known beforehand how it would be received. He tasted; why did He even taste? Was it as an act of condescension, of gratitude for a kindly deed? He was always courteous; He would not spurn an act of kindness even on an occasion such as this. But He would not drink; not in spite of His maddening thirst; that He should do so to avoid the coming pain is unthinkable. "The chalice which My Father hath given Me, shall I not drink it?" And to do so, that He may drink it to the dregs, He must resist the soothing chalice offered Him by man. There is something peculiarly strong, even while it is peculiarly agonizing, in this rejection of the cup that is already touching His lips. If we could only have the same strength!

3. The only other fact noted is the company in which He was crucified. "Two other male-factors," says our translation, as if the Greek idiom best fitted the occasion—"two other male-factors," implying that He was already one. Indeed, "with the wicked He was reputed." St. John cannot resist calling attention to the exact fulfilment of this prophecy. It is true this charge against Him was soon set aside; with Pilate it had not the least weight; nevertheless, at the very end, King or no King, Son of God or only son of man, sedition-monger or not, it was after the manner of criminals and in the company of criminals that He was actually put to death. Truly, as St. Paul says, "He was made sin." Nowhere does Our Lord come nearer to man than when He so submits to be nailed down to earth among them. St. Paul again and again dwells upon the simple fact. In his Eastern way he dwells affectionately, almost fancifully, on its manifold significance. And the Church has clung with both her arms round the foot of that cross ever since, while the drip of the blood has fallen unceasingly upon her.

Summary

1. The hill of Calvary, the most sacred spot in the world.
2. "When He had tasted, He would not drink."
3. Our Lord died with malefactors, and as one of them.

XXXIX.—THE TITLE

"And Pilate wrote a title also, and he put it upon the cross over His head. And the writing was: This is Jesus of Nazareth, the King of the Jews. This title, therefore, many of the Jews read, because the place where Jesus was crucified was near to the city, and it was written in Hebrew, in Greek, and in Latin. Then the chief priests of the Jews said to Pilate: Write not, The King of the Jews, but that He said, I am the King of the Jews. Pilate answered: What I have written I have written."—Matt. xxvii. 37; Mark xv. 26; Luke xxiii. 38; John xix. 19-22.

1. The sentence had been pronounced, and had been promptly carried out; no time had been allowed for reflection or for cooler judgment; the chief priests had seen to this, as the Devil sees to it when he has once won the soul to consent to grievous sin. The only thing that Pilate would now do was to justify himself in the eyes of all the world; the world was his judge, not God, nor truth, of which he affected to know nothing. So he wrote with his own hand the "title," "in Hebrew, in Greek, and in Latin," so that all the world might know. "This is Jesus of Nazareth," the man from turbulent Galilee, from despised Nazareth, who had of late disturbed the peace of Jerusalem, and had made Himself a trouble to authority. "This is the King of the Jews," the one thing of which He had been convicted; before Pilate himself He had said: "Thou sayest that I am a King";

121

and though He had not said, "I am King of
the Jews," though He had added, "My kingdom
is not from hence," though Pilate had known
for certain that His Kingship would not clash
with the authority of Caesar, still, the half-truth
must be proclaimed that the execution might
be justified. The world is ruled by half-truths.

2. But this was not enough for His enemies.
Pilate may have sentenced Him on the ground
that He made Himself a King, but they had
done Him to death "because He made Himself
the Son of God." Either Our Lord was the
"King of the Jews" or He was not. If He was,
then He was also Messias, and Messias was
the Son of David, and the Son of David was
the Son of God. If He was not, then He would
have been put to death, not by Jewish law,
which had no such sentence, but by Roman law
alone; and the chief priests would be exculpated.
To leave the "title" as it stood might set the
people thinking; they might argue along the
line we have just mentioned, and the conclusion
might make "the last state worse than the first."

3. But Pilate was unmoved, unmoved with the
desperation of one who knows he has done great
wrong, and who turns in hate upon those who
have driven him to it. He knew he had done
wrong; he knew that now they were saying in
their hearts: "What is that to us? Look you
to it." He knew, too, on Our Lord's own evidence
that "they who have delivered Me to thee have

the greater sin"; therefore, if he could he would deprive them of their palm of victory. He would thwart them if he could, insult them if he could; if this "title" did not please them, then all the more would he insist upon it. But why did it not please them? "He knew that for envy they had delivered Him." Their very fear showed that the man was their King, and that they knew it. Then, let come what might, he had saved himself in the eyes of the world; he had left them guilty and responsible; he would leave written what he had written.

Summary

1. Pilate called Him "King of the Jews" to save his own reputation.
2. The chief priests resented it for fear of theirs.
3. Pilate found satisfaction in turning on those who had led him into crime.

XL.—THE FIRST WORD; THE GARMENTS

"And Jesus said: Father, forgive them, for they know not what they do. Then the soldiers, after they had crucified Him, took His garments (and they made four parts, to every soldier a part, casting lots upon them what every man should take), and also His coat. Now the coat was without seam, woven from the top throughout. They said then to one another: Let us not cut it, but let us cast lots for it, whose it shall be; that the word might be fulfilled which was spoken by the prophet: They have parted My garments among them, and upon My vesture they have cast lots. And the soldiers indeed did these things. And it was the third hour, and

they crucified Him."—Matt. xxvii. 35; Mark xv. 24
25; Luke xxiii. 34; John xix. 23, 24.

1. Our Lord appears to have spoken the first
of His seven words, recorded only by St. Luke
while He was yet being nailed to the cross. We
know how excessive torture has wrung prayer
from the lips of martyrs and other sufferers
who have found in the effort some counteracting
power to endure. So it had been with Him in
the Garden. And now, at this last act in the
drama, His prayer is the spontaneous expression
of that which is deepest in his heart. Whatever
else Our Lord is, the deepest thing in Him is
forgiveness. He had offered it to Peter, and it
had been accepted; to Annas, to Caiphas, and
most of all to Pilate, and it had been ignored
new He includes all in his offer, for if His
executioners are prayed for at such a moment
then what soul may not hope? "Not for the
world do I pray, but for those whom Thou hast
given Me out of the world," He had said but
the evening before. And now He lets us see
how far His prayer extends. It is as though
He said: "Not for the world do I pray, which
is a dominating spirit; but for every individual
soul that is in the world, and that I would
gladly rescue from it."

2. The dividing of the garments is mentioned
by each of the Evangelists, but is elaborated by
St. John. Through the last scenes of the tragedy, St. John has his eye fixed upon prophecy

and its fulfilment. He seems to be asking himself, Why all this? And he finds his answer in the unity of all revelation. To St. John, St. Augustine is a perfect antithesis; for as the first unites the past with the event, St. Augustine unites in it all the future. St. John sees in the saving of the seamless garment the fulfilment of the past; the other sees the prophecy of that which is to come. To the end of time the enemies of Our Lord will crucify Him. They will rob Him of His garments and divide His worldly possessions among them. But His seamless garment, the Church herself, they will never divide; she shall remain intact, though they appropriate her for their own.

3. "And the soldiers indeed did these things," concludes St. John. "And it was the third hour, and they crucified Him," concludes St. Mark. It was in the middle of the day, in the sight of all the world, with the greatest publicity that was possible, that Our Lord was put to death; not in a secluded prison-yard, with just the official witnesses present and no more, and with all the care that modern humanity demands. We look on the sight; we are fascinated by it to this day, this bleeding body of Our Lord, the stream from which overflows and drowns all the world; we hear Him say, "I, being lifted up, will draw all things to Myself," and we watch "all things" yielding, gradually, gradually, to the fascination.

125

Summary

1. He prayed for His enemies.
2. His garments were divided, but His seamless robe was not parted.
3. He was crucified in the sight of all the world.

XLI.—THE MOCKERY

"And they sat down and watched Him. And the people stood beholding. And they that passed by blasphemed Him, wagging their heads and saying: Vah, Thou who destroyest the Temple of God, and in three days buildest it up again, save Thy own self; if Thou be the Son of God, come down from the cross. In like manner the chief priests with the scribes and ancients, mocking, derided Him, saying: He saved others, Himself He cannot save. If He be Christ the King of Israel, if He be Christ the Son of God, let Him now come down from the cross, that we may see and believe. He trusted in God; let Him now deliver Him, if He will have Him, for He said: I am the Son of God."—Matt. xxvii. 36-44; Mark xv. 29-32; Luke xxiii. 35-37.

1. With those whose consciences are not yet hardened by iniquity, with ordinary children and young people, with grown-up men and women who have lived to be true, a great sin committed has a certain paralyzing effect. The poor sinner rises up from it as if dazed; he has lost something, he can scarcely know what; it seems to him that henceforth life must be another thing; the sun, the air, the flowers of the field, seem to accuse him; the laugh is off his lip, the brilliance faded from his eye, the very skin of his body seems swarth and shiny; having done

126

hat which is the degradation of a man, his
very manhood seems to have oozed from him.
t is true of the individual; it is true of an
inhuman crowd; and as "they sat and watched
Him," and "the people stood beholding," we
seem to find the paralyzing sense of guilt and
clamminess coming over those around the cross,
silent and condemning.

2. Of course, to remain under the spell is not
to be endured. It will lead either to despair or
to contrition. Since perfect happiness has been
forfeited, which can rest only on the peace of
a good conscience, then happiness of another
kind must be secured. Conscience must be buried
in confusion, its voice must be silenced by up-
roar; the sinner and his accomplices must clam-
or themselves out of their stupor into the new
life to which they have doomed themselves. So
we see them always doing; so we see them here.
The spell is broken; "they passed by blaspheming, wagging their heads"; "in like manner the
chief priests with the scribes and ancients,
mocking, deriding Him"; cowards before, they
are now more brutal cowards still, putting a bold
face on their shame, a howling laughter above
their misery—one knows the type too well.

3. But the language is beyond mistake; in
moments of strong passion the secrets of the
heart appear. "If Thou be the Son of God,
save Thy own self." That is at the root of all.
The fear that indeed He is that is not yet dead.

"If He be Christ, the King of Israel, if He be Christ, the Son of God, let Him come down from the cross, that we may see and believe." Could anyone have uttered such a cry who did not already in his heart believe? "He saved others, Himself He cannot save." Another confession, even as was that in the better days: "Because of Thy good works we blame Thee not, but because Thou, being but a man, dost make Thyself the Son of God." Dear Lord, how this self-condemning cry has rung through the world ever since. We accept Christ as our doer of good, we accept Him as a Prophet, we condone "Hosanna to the Son of David"; but Son of God He shall not be! If He makes that claim, then all His very deeds shall be turned against Him.

Summary

1. The paralysis of the guilty crowd.
2. The recovery in noise and confusion.
3. The language of their abuse.

XLII.—THE PENITENT THIEF

"And the soldiers also mocked Him, coming to Him and offering Him vinegar and saying: If Thou be the King of the Jews, save Thyself. And the selfsame thing the thieves also that were crucified with Him reproached Him with, and reviled Him. And one of these robbers who were hanging, blasphemed Him, saying: If Thou be Christ, save Thyself and us. But the other, answering, rebuked him, saying: Neither dost thou fear God, seeing thou art under the same condemnation? And we, indeed, just

128

*y, for we receive the due reward of our deeds; but
his man hath done no evil. And he said to Jesus:
Lord, remember me when Thou shalt come into Thy
Kingdom. And Jesus said to him: Amen, I say to
thee, this day thou shalt be with Me in Paradise."*—
Matt. xxvii. 44; Mark xv. 32; Luke xxiii. 36-43.

1. It is easy to meditate upon this scene in
the Passion. The soldiers are of little account;
they act as do those of their class, with no
opinion of their own, but catching at that which
pleases authority. Hence the terms of their
abuse; being Roman soldiers, the "King of the
Jews" has no meaning to them, but evidently
it has some supernatural meaning to the chief
priests; hence they bid Him "save Himself,"
which to a Roman would be a foolish taunt.
With the thieves it might be different. They
at least were Jews, even if they had long since
laid aside all thought of religion; from their
lips the taunt is akin to that from the lips of
those who have once had the faith, but have
it no longer, and who, having lost it, and having
a consequence lost much more beside, then cry
it against faith as being a delusion and bank-
rupt. They thrust Our Lord aside; they deliberately choose their own path; then they take
his as proof that He is not.

2. But often such people find their best rival
among themselves. One will rise up who will
have at least the humility to recognize his own
guilt; whether there is Christ or not, at least

he himself has only got his own deserts; whether there is Christ or not, at least there is a just God. This leads to another recognition: that of injustice done to others. Whether this is Christ or not, at least He is not guilty as we are. Thus there are three steps, seen often enough in ordinary life. The man who has done wrong and will acknowledge it, will find the discovery of God not difficult. The discovery of God will soon adjust his attitude to others; and this will make his duty to them easy.

3. Then comes the climax. There may be many ways to the discovery of Our Lord, but none is so easy, none so illuminating, as that of the penitent thief. He is not taught by books; it is not proved to him by argument; it begins with the defense of a good man: "This man hath done no evil." On the contrary, this man hath done nothing but good. Therefore this man's word is to be trusted. On the contrary all that is evil is ranged against Him; it has done Him to death, it has numbered Him with ourselves. And meanwhile He does nothing; He says nothing; He dies without a word, without defense. Who can this man be, with Whom is all that is good, against Whom is all that is evil, Whose death alone will satisfy the world? The truth flashes on him; he cries out: "Lord remember me," and he receives in reply instant canonization. In spite of all the suffering, the "Amen, I say to thee, this day thou shalt be

130

with Me in Paradise," was a moment of pure
joy for Our Lord.

Summary

1. The abuse of the soldiers and the two thieves.
2. The growth of grace in the heart of the good
thief.
3. And its reward.

XLIII.—MARY AND JOHN

*"Now there stood by the cross of Jesus His Mother,
and His Mother's sister, Mary of Cleophas, and Mary
Magdalene. When Jesus therefore saw His Mother,
and the disciple standing whom He loved, He saith to
His Mother: Woman, behold thy son. After that
He saith to the disciple: Behold thy Mother. And
from that hour the disciple took her to his own."—
John xix. 25-27.*

1. Of all the scenes in the Passion, there is
one more familiar to every one of us than
this. The crowd has dwindled away; even its
noisy exultation has not been able to keep up
its false courage for long. There remain a few,
waiting to see the end; but these, no doubt,
are not those who have been most violent; they
are the partially sympathetic, the more or less
faithful remnant, the curious. There remains,
too, the guard, mainly of Roman soldiers, divided
between contempt for the Victim and contempt
for the people who have made such a display
of their Eastern ferocity. It is true these soldiers have played their part in the cruelty; but
they are Western souls, they are more easily

sated in their lust for blood, and they stand
there sullen and disgusted. Instinctively, without
themselves noticing it, the true mourners have
crept closer and closer; the guard does not
trouble to prevent them; they find some comfort
for themselves in this act of mercy. So three
women stand there—Mary Immaculate, Mary the
Penitent, Mary the mother of Apostles.

2. There is also at least one more—"the disciple whom He loved." St. John, in thus speaking
of himself, does not mean that Our Lord did
not love others also; he does not mean that
he was himself loved more than others; it is
enough for him to know that in matter of fact
he is loved, and has been given tokens of deep
love, whatever else may have been given to
others. Peter also was a "disciple whom He
loved"; the last scene recorded by St. John at
the end of his Gospel is a great proof of this;
but the same might be said of them all, of us
all. It is not a little thing to stand at the foot
of the cross, and to know that I can describe
myself, in spite of all my cowardice, my deser-
tions, my denials, my treacheries, as "the disciple standing whom He loved."

3. Jesus saw them from the cross. Consider
the simple fact. Fastened as He was, the physical effort to look at anything must have been
an additional torture; one has seen a semblance
of it on a death-bed of torture. In such agony
as He was, the effort to think of others was a

132

wonder of charity; we forgive much disregard
from those who are in intense suffering. But
Jesus saw them; He saw that motionless Mother;
He knew that for her His death must naturally
mean her own; that her love and her life were
so linked with His that when He died she too
would fade and die. But He would not have
it so. He would yet have her to live, for she
had a work to do; "that out of many hearts
thoughts might be revealed." She must be given
another object of her Mother's love, another
child to cherish in place of the one she was
losing. There was John; there was all mankind;
let her take him and them. "Woman, behold thy
son." And if so, then let John, let all men, do
to her as He Himself had done: "Man, behold
thy Mother."

Summary

1. There stood by the cross of Jesus the soldiers
and the three Marys.

2. There stood also the disciple whom He loved.

3. He gave Mary to the disciple, and the disciple
to Mary.

XLIV.—THE FOURTH WORD

*"And when the sixth hour was come, there was
darkness over the whole earth until the ninth hour.
And about the ninth hour Jesus cried out with a
loud voice, saying: Eloi, Eloi, lamma sabacthani?
Which is, being interpreted: My God, My God, why
hast Thou forsaken Me? And some of them that
stood there and heard, said: Behold, this man calleth
for Elias."*—Matt. xxvii. 45-47; Mark xv. 33-35;
Luke xxiii. 44.

1. "From the sixth to the ninth hour." The darkness is clearly miraculous; the disciples understood it as such. But it was such a miracle as the enemy could easily assert to be not proven. Such is the way of God. Miracles are more usually for those who have the wish to believe; for those who have the wish to disbelieve it is always possible to find a way out, even if it be the crude answer that we do not understand all the facts. There is often darkness at midday; that on this occasion it should have fitted in with Our Lord's hanging on the cross is a coincidence. But we understand; Nature held her veil before her face in very shame at what was being done. She would not see; she would have others not see. Our Lord had said that if the children who praised Him were silenced, the very stones would cry out; now all Nature cries out at the crime that is committed. And all the time we must not forget the three long, long hours of Our Lord's last agony.

2. "My God, My God, why hast Thou forsaken Me?" The words open the Twenty-first Psalm. But it would seem to be a mistake to suppose that they are merely that and no more. Rather they are an apt quotation used to express Our Lord's real state of soul; they are another fulfilment of prophecy. Our Lord is drinking the cup to the dregs; He is deliberately going through the "hour and the power of darkness," and He wills that He should be deprived of this

last consolation. From other passages it is clear that Our Lord's mind, like Our Lady's, is full of the Old Testament and its texts, which come familiarly to the mind in time of prayer, even as ejaculations come to the mind of one who has made himself familiar with them. Hence now, in the moment of His great desolation, the desolation of the Psalmist, prophetic of His own, provides Him with this form of prayer. If Our Lord was tempted by the Devil after His long fast in the desert, if then the Devil only "left Him for a time," we need not be surprised if now temptation of this strange kind oppresses Him.

3. The Psalm which He cites is one of the great prophetic psalms, and therefore deserves to be considered here. Here are some of its passages:

"But I—a worm and no man:
The reproach of men, and the outcast of the
    people.
All they that saw Me laughed Me to scorn;
    Curled their lips and wagged their head.
'He hopes in the Lord, let Him deliver Him;
Let Him save Him, seeing He delighteth in Him!'"

And again

"I am poured out like water;
And all My bones are numbered.
My heart is become like wax within My breast.
My tongue is dried up as a potsherd,
    Cleaving to My mouth:
    And Thou hast reduced Me to the dust of death.
For dogs have encompassed Me:

A council of the malignant hath besieged Me.
They have dug My hands and My feet.
   They have numbered all my bones.
They have looked and gloated with their eyes upon
   Me.
   They parted My garments among them:
   And upon My vesture they cast lots."

Summary

1. The darkness from the sixth to the ninth hour.
2. "My God, My God, why hast Thou forsaken
Me?"
3. Psalm Twenty-one.

XLV.—THE FIFTH AND SIXTH WORDS

*"Afterwards Jesus, knowing that all things were
accomplished, that the Scripture might be fulfilled,
said: I thirst. Now there was a vessel set there full
of vinegar. And immediately one of them, running,
took a sponge and filled it with vinegar and put it
on a reed about hyssop, and offered it to His mouth,
and gave Him to drink. And others said: Stay, let
us see whether Elias will come to take Him down
and deliver Him. When Jesus therefore had taken
the vinegar He said: It is consummated."—Matt.
xxvii. 48, 49; Mark xv. 36; John xix. 28-30.*

1. His last word was a quotation from a
psalm; in this He refers to another, Psalm Sixty-
eight. This, like the Twenty-first, is full of
prophetic allusion, and Our Lord's quotation of
it seems to invite us to mingle our thoughts
with His at this moment. Let us, then, take
some passages. First the prophet sees the deluge
which overwhelms Him:

"Save Me, O God; for there cometh
    The water even unto My soul....
I am come beneath the deeps of water,
    And the flood overwhelms Me....
My eyes have grown dim from hoping
    In God, my God.
More than are the hairs upon My head
    Are those who hate Me without cause."

2. Then, later, He gives the reason of the enmity, His very effort to do good.

"I am become a stranger to My brethren,
    And an alien to the sons of My mother.
Because the zeal of Thy house hath eaten Me up,
    And the reproaches of Thy reproachers have
      fallen on Me.
I humbled My soul in fasting,
    And it was made a reproach to Me.
I made haircloth My garment,
    And I became a byword to them.
They that sat in the gate spoke against Me,
    And the wine-bibbers made Me their song.
But as for Me, My prayer is to Thee:
    Let mercy one day come."

3. Then comes the second part of this great Psalm: the strong appeal:

"O God, in the multitude of Thy mercy hear Me,
    Deliver Me from them that hate Me!
In the truth of Thy salvation draw Me from the
      mire,
    And out of the deep waters!
Let not the flood of water drown Me,
    Nor the deep swallow Me up!
Let Me not sink, nor let close over Me
    The mouth of the pit!
Hear Me, O Lord, for Thy mercy is kind
    For I am in trouble.
Look upon Me in the greatness of Thy tender
      heart,

Make haste to hear Me.
Come near to My soul and deliver it,
    Save Me because of My enemies."

And this is followed by the prophecy:

"Thou knowest My reproach,
    My confusion and My shame are in Thy sight.
All they, My oppressors, deride Me,
    My heart is broken and in misery.
I looked for compassion, but in vain,
    For comfort, and I found none.
They gave Me gall for My food,
    And in My thirst they gave Me vinegar to
        drink."

He would see this last prophecy fulfilled before
He died; now all is done; He has finished the
work God gave Him to do.

Summary

1. Our Lord throws us back to the prophecy of
Psalm Sixty-eight: first the trouble.

2. Then its cause; He suffers because of His zeal
for His Father's house.

3. Then the effect upon Himself; the treatment
at the hands of His enemies.

XLVI.—THE DEATH OF OUR LORD

*"And Jesus again crying with a loud voice said:
Father, into Thy hands I commend My spirit. And
saying this, bowing down His head, He gave up the
ghost. And behold the sun was darkened, and the
veil of the Temple was rent in two in the midst from
the top even to the bottom, and the earth quaked,
and the rocks were rent. And the graves were
opened, and many bodies of the saints that had slept
arose, and coming out of the tombs after His
resurrection, came into the holy city and appeared*

138

to many."—Matt. xxvii. 50-53; Mark xv. 37, 38;
Luke xxiii. 45, 46; John xix. 31.

1. Again, and for the last time, does our
dying Lord take His words from the Psalms.
The Psalms are His dying prayers. In this last
word, from the Thirtieth Psalm, He seems to
suggest to us our own thoughts and prayers
as we watch Him dying and after He is dead.
We may, then, well take it as such. First, we
may well imagine, is His own last prayer:

"In Thee, O Lord, have I hoped,
　　Let Me never be confounded.
In Thy justice deliver and free Me,
　　Bow down Thine ear to Me,
Be to Me a protecting rock,
　　A house of refuge to save Me.
For Thou art My strength and My refuge,
　　And for Thy Name's sake Thou wilt lead Me.
Thou dost nourish Me, and save Me from the
　　　　snare,
　　Which they have hidden for Me.
Yea, O Lord, Thou art My protector,
　　Into Thy hands I commend My spirit."

2. "And saying this, bowing down His head,
He gave up the ghost." But we, as we do by
the bedside of one who dies before our eyes,
carry on our prayer with the same Psalm, one
of mingled joy and sorrow. For it goes on:

"But I have hoped in the Lord,
　　I will be glad and rejoice in Thy mercy.
For Thou hast regarded My lowliness,
　　Thou hast saved My soul out of distress.
Thou hast not enclosed Me in the hands of the
　　　　enemy,
　　Thou hast set My feet in a spacious place.

*　　　*　　　*　　　*　　　*

139

I have trusted in Thee, O Lord,
    I said: 'Thou art My God.
My lots are in Thy hand; deliver Me
    From the hands of My foes, My persecutors.'
Make Thy face to shine upon Thy servant;
    Save Me in Thy mercy.
Let Me not be confounded, O Lord, for I have
      called on Thee."

3. The Psalm concludes with that refrain of trust which every holy death-bed inspires, but which must most of all be inspired by this holiest death-bed of all.

"How great is Thy sweetness, O Lord,
    Which Thou hast hidden for them that fear
      Thee;
Which Thou hast wrought for them that hope in
    Thee,
    In the sight of the sons of men
Thou dost shield them with the shield of Thy
      countenance
    From the disturbance of men.
Thou dost protect them in Thy tabernacle
    From the contradiction of tongues.
Blessed be the Lord, Who hath shown His great
      mercy to Me
    In a fortified city.
I said in the depression of My mind:
    'I am cast away before Thine eyes.'
Then Thou hast heard the voice of My prayer
    When I cried to Thee.
O love the Lord, all ye His saints,
    Who keep the truth of the Lord.

*   *   *   *   *

Do ye manfully, and let your heart be strength-
    ened,
    All ye that hope in the Lord."

Summary
1. Our Lord's last prayer: trust in God.
2. Our prayer beside His body: trust in God.
3. With thanksgiving.

XLVII.—THE CENTURION'S CONFESSION

"Now the centurion, who stood over against Him, and they that were with him watching Jesus, seeing that crying out in this manner He had given up the ghost, having seen the earthquake and the things that were done, were greatly afraid, and glorified God, saying: Indeed this was a just man. Indeed this was the Son of God. Indeed this man was the Son of God."—Matt. xxvii. 54; Mark xv. 39; Luke xxiii. 47.

1. Here, when all is over, we have, as it were, the verdict of an irresponsible jury. It is not necessary to suppose that they understood the full significance of the title, but the words had been ringing in their ears since the beginning of the tragedy, and their conclusion was that, whatever they might imply, He had vindicated His cause against His murderers. The evidence may not have been convincing to a cold materialist; it was apparently no more than that He had died with a loud cry on His lips, that the earth had quaked, that the sky had darkened, and that other strange things had happened. But behind all these were other details, far more convincing in themselves, yet useless to the mind of the materialist: the revolting passion of the victors contrasted with the calm dignity of the

141

Victim; the infuriated mob that supported the murderers contrasted with the quiet sorrow of Our Lord's followers; the self-dissatisfaction of the first in their hour of triumph, and the confident "Into Thy hands I commend My spirit" of the second, at His moment of utterest defeat. By these marks is He known; by these marks is the persecuted truth known in all ages.

2. So we have the proof anticipated in the Old Testament; the real sign of the Son of God was this. Thus the Psalmist, speaking prophetically, says: "I am a worm and no man: the reproach of men, and the outcast of the people. All they that saw Me have laughed Me to scorn: they have spoken with the lips, and wagged the head. He hoped in the Lord, let Him deliver Him: let Him save Him, seeing He delighteth in Him." And Isaias: "There is no beauty in Him, nor comeliness: and we have seen Him, and there was no sightliness, that we should be desirous of Him. Despised, and the most abject of men, a man of sorrows, and acquainted with infirmity." And Jeremias: "I was as a meek lamb that is carried to be a victim: and I knew not that they had devised counsels against Me, saying: Let us put wood on His bread, and cut Him off from the land of the living, and let His name be remembered no more." If the Jews had remembered this side of prophecy, "they would not have crucified the Lord of Glory."

3. But there is the more significant prophecy

still, which may well occupy our thoughts at the foot of the cross. The wicked in the Book of Wisdom say: "He boasteth that He hath the knowledge of God, and calleth Himself the Son of God. He is become a censurer of our thoughts. He is grievous unto us, even to behold: for His life is not like other men's, and His ways are very different. We are esteemed by Him as triflers, and He abstaineth from our ways as from filthiness, and He preferreth the latter end of the just, and glorieth that He hath God for His Father. Let us see, then, if His words be true, and let us prove what will happen to Him, and we shall know what His end shall be. For if He be the true Son of God, He will defend Him, and will deliver Him from the hand of His enemies. Let us examine Him by outrages and tortures, that we may know His meekness and try His patience. Let us condemn Him to a most shameful death; for there shall be respect had unto Him by His words."

Summary

1. The centurion's evidence of the Son of God.
2. and 3. The evidence of prophecy.

XLVIII.—THE MOURNERS

"And all the multitude of them that were come together to that sight, and saw the things that were done, returned striking their breasts. And there were also women, among whom was Mary Magdalene, and Mary the Mother of James the less, and of

*Joseph, and Salome, and the mother of the sons of
Zebedee, who also when He was in Galilee followed
Him, and ministered to Him, and many other women
that came up with Him to Jerusalem. And all his
acquaintances and the women stood afar off beholding these things."*—Matt. xxvii. 55, 56; Mark xv.
40, 41; Luke xxiii. 48, 49.

1. "All the multitude of them that were come
together to that sight." So this was a "sight,"
a show, a spectacle, this murder of the Son of
God! And a great "multitude" had come to
witness it! Of whom was that multitude com-
posed? We have heard the crowd crying out its
ridicule and blasphemies as He lay bleeding to
death; are these the same people that now go
back, "striking their breasts"? It is scarcely
credible, though perhaps some were in the number; just as, with all great sin, the sense of
remorse at the moment of achievement overtakes
the sense of satisfaction in the sin, and turns
the cup of pleasure into bitterness. This bitterness some take for contrition, but it is not that;
it is the physical and moral reaction, and is
the natural basis upon which true contrition may
be built. Possibly in the case of these poor
Jews the sense of remorse endured, the fruits
of which were to be reaped by St. Peter after
Pentecost.

2. But the words seem to imply that besides
the murderers and their mob following was
another "multitude" standing outside, of merely
curious spectators; and on these in His last

144

moments Our Lord had pity. They had been passive all the time, but their very silent acquiescence had told against Him. They again confirm the truth, witnessed to by the history of the world, that the "multitude" is usually little guilty of the great crimes against God that are committed; it is the leaders who provoke the crime that "have the greater sin." Hence we often hear in Scripture that Our Lord "had pity on the multitude"; that He was "filled with compassion" for it; that He drew it after Him; and here He gives it sorrow for its share in the evil that has been done.

3. And somewhere in this crowd, unmolested by anyone, probably pitied, perhaps by their presence and behavior stirring in those around sorrow and sympathy for Our Lord, is the group of faithful women, so pointedly mentioned by the Evangelists, who had followed Him in Galilee, and had ministered to His wants, and had thus, under His direction, laid the foundation of the work of women in the Church, trained in some sense by Our Lord Himself, even as had been the Apostles. These now had been rewarded for their faithful service by being given their special place on Calvary; and for all time will be honored and imitated by other faithful women-servants of Our Lord, who in their turn will be rewarded by a share in the Crucifixion—women in the world, women in religion, saints marked with the insignia of the Passion—a

Gertrude, a Catherine, a Theresa. They did nothing; they only stood and looked on; but their presence must have been no small joy to Our Lord in His last hour.

Summary

1. The remorse of the first group.
2. The contrition of the second group.
3. The sorrow and sympathy of the third group.

XLIX.—THE PIERCED SIDE

"Then the Jews (because it was the Parasceve), that the bodies might not remain upon the cross on the Sabbath-day (for that was a great Sabbath-day). besought Pilate that their legs might be broken, and that they might be taken away. The soldiers therefore came, and they broke the legs of the first, and of the other that was crucified with Him. But when they came to Jesus, and saw that He was already dead, they did not break His legs, but one of the soldiers opened his side with a spear, and immediately there came out blood and water. And he that saw gave testimony, and his testimony is true. And he knoweth that he saith true, that you also may believe. For these things were done that the Scripture might be fulfilled: You shall not break a bone of Him. And again another Scripture saith: They shall look on Him Whom they pierced."—John xix. 31-37.

1. Jesus is dead, but His two companions are not yet, and the great Sabbath-day is drawing near. St. John, with his eye kept steadily fixed in the great unity of the work of God among

146

men, that unity which he was able the better
to recognize after the vision of the Apocalypse,
that unity which we shall understand in the
great revelation of the next world, reminds us
of two great though insignificant details, which
might well be the key to many more. "They did
not break His legs;" they broke no bone of the
"Lamb that was slain from the beginning of
the world." Thus was obeyed the precept con-
cerning the Paschal Lamb: "You shall not break
a bone of Him." The membership of the Body
of Christ must be a complete thing; to the end
of time a "severed limb" shall be a contradiction.

2. Thus for the fulfilment of the past. But
the last of the prophets had spoken another
word looking into the future. In one of the
most difficult passages of the Old Testament the
prophet Zachary had strangely intermingled
words of triumph and of sorrow. The day would
come when "Jerusalem" would revive, when "the
Lord" would "protect the inhabitants of Jerusalem," even from herself; and the prophet goes
on: "And I will pour out upon the house of
David, and upon the inhabitants of Jerusalem,
the spirit of grace and of prayers: and they
shall look upon Me, Whom they have pierced:
and they shall mourn for Him as one mourneth
for an only son, and they shall grieve over Him,
as the manner is to grieve for the death of the
first-born." St. John saw the heart of Jesus
Christ pierced through; he remembers the word

of Zachary; he knows that the piercing of that heart means many things for Christ's own that are to be.

3. Here St. John reverts to that form of emphasis which we find in two or three other places of his writings. We find it at the beginning of his Epistles; we find it at the end of the Apocalypse; we find it at the conclusion of his Gospel, where he says: "These are written that you may believe that Jesus is the Christ, the Son of God: and that believing you may have life in His name." And here he says: "He knoweth that he saith true, that you also may believe." What would he have us believe from this passage? That Jesus Christ is indeed the fulfilment of all prophecy; that He is the great Sacrifice, concluding in Himself all that has gone before; that He has poured Himself out, to the last drop of blood and water; that henceforth, for all time and for all eternity, the stream springing from Calvary shall flow on, preserving innocence in many, cleansing many more, so that the glory of Heaven itself shall consist in being steeped in the Blood of the Lamb.

Summary

1. No bone was broken.
2. The side was opened.
3. The great meaning of this for all time.

L.—THE GIFT OF THE BODY

"And when evening was come (because it was the Parasceve, that is, the day before the Sabbath) a certain rich man of Arimathea, a city of Judaea, by name Joseph, who was a senator, a noble councillor, a good and just man, who also himself waited for the Kingdom of God, and was a disciple of Jesus, but in private, for fear of the Jews; this man had not consented to their counsel and doings; went in boldly to Pilate and besought that he might take away the body of Jesus. But Pilate wondered that He should be already dead. And when he had understood it by the centurion, he commanded that the body of Jesus should be delivered to Joseph. He came therefore and took away the body of Jesus."—Matt. xxvii. 57-59; Mark xv. 42-45; Luke xxiii. 50-52; John xix. 38.

1. The body of Jesus Christ must be disposed of, the body which has saved the world! Unless something is done for it by men, it will be thrown away into the common criminals' pit, as so many bodies of His martyrs have been thrown away. But for us it matters little; His body must not be treated so. The occasion makes the hero. Joseph of Arimathea has hitherto been no man of action. He has lived his honored life alone, a life that has for the most part been spent in smooth waters, respected by friend and enemy, moderate, prudent, committing himself in little or nothing. But now the time for the one deed of his life has come, and he is equal to it. For how many—perhaps for the majority of people—is life a preparation for, does life center itself in, a single heroic deed!

2. In this precisely does Joseph of Arimathea contrast with Pilate. He, too, had his single chance, his one critical moment in life, and he failed. And now that all is over "Pilate wondered that He should be already dead." We may with reason wonder that he wondered. He knew all Our Lord had endured. He knew that no ordinary man could have gone through it all and lived. His enemies had feared that His life would ebb out on the road to Calvary, before He had been nailed to the cross. But with Pilate the wish was father to the thought. From the beginning he has hoped that he himself would be "innocent of the blood of this just man." He had tried to throw the responsibility on others; he had himself turned and writhed many ways; and he had hoped that this "King of the Jews" might at the very last yet "come down from the cross" and save His reputation and Pilate's. But now he hears the doom; the heart of the dead Jesus Christ has been pierced through; there is no hope; whatever men may say, whatever he himself may affect, he is the murderer of "this just man."

3. One's heart aches for Pilate, as it must ache for any soul that awakes to grievous sin, and hears the voice ringing in its ears: "What hast thou done?" He cannot restore that life. He cannot ever again restore his own life. But there is sorrow mingled with the remorse in the concession that is made to Joseph. Poor

Jesus Christ! Though the Council has condemned
Him and done Him to death, at least the most
honorable member of the Council shall bury
Him. Though He is so poor Himself that the
soldiers shall have His clothes, and His very
body shall be a thing to be given away, yet it
shall be buried with the honor that is its due.
What a host of mystical thoughts are contained
in this gift of Our Lord's body by man to man!

Summary
1. The one opportunity in his life for Joseph of
Arimathea is accepted, as with Simon of Cyrene.
2. The contrast between him and Pilate.
3. The body of Our Lord is given by man to man.

LI.—THE BURIAL

*"And Nicodemus also came, who at first came to
Jesus by night, bringing a mixture of myrrh and
aloes, about a hundred pound. They took therefore
the body of Jesus, and buying fine linen, wrapped
it up in the linen cloths with the spices, as it is the
custom with the Jews to bury. And there was in
the place where He was crucified a garden, and in
the garden a new sepulchre, his own (Joseph's)
monument, which he had hewed out in a rock, wherein never yet any man had been laid. There therefore, by reason of the Parasceve of the Jews, they
laid Jesus, because the sepulchre was nigh at hand.
And he rolled a great stone to the door of the monument, and went his way. And Mary Magdalene,
and Mary the mother of Joseph, and the women that
were come with Him from Galilee, following after,
sitting over against the sepulchre, beheld where His
body was laid. And returning they prepared spices*

151

and ointments, and on the Sabbath-day they rested,
according to the commandment."—Matt. xxvii. 59-61;
Mark xv. 46, 47; Luke xxiii. 53-56; John xix. 39-42.

1. There is something striking, one might say
pathetic, in watching the chief mourners in Our
Lord's funeral procession. We have not Peter,
the first and the leader of His own, but Joseph
of Arimathea, who, in status at least, belonged
to the camp of His enemies. We have not any
of those who had been seen with Him always,
but Nicodemus, who feared ever to be seen with
Him at all. The others provided nothing for
the funeral; even John was occupied with other
things; these provided of their reverent labor. There cannot but be deep significance in
this; may one not call it the consecration of
the layman's work in the Church? The provision,
that is, of the material things and the material
labor that are needful for the due honor that
belongs to the Body of Christ, corporal and
mystical.

2. The sepulchre, again, is a matter for
thought. Half an hour before who would have
imagined that "this malefactor" would have received so honorable a place of burial? Yet He
is given, not merely a place of honor, but the
very best that Jewry could provide; for it is
a tomb specially prepared, in a special place, and
in a special way, by a noble member of the
Council for himself. And He is buried, not
merely with due Jewish rites, but in the richest

way that a rich and noble Jew could arrange. Instinctively one's thoughts go towards the Blessed Sacrament. No matter what insult is offered to it. the Body of Christ is now and always the object of the most lavish gifts of man. Things perishable and things imperishable, myrrh and aloes, or the tomb, alike are bestowed upon it to overflowing; and no one who understands will dream of calling it waste.

3. We look again when all is over. Joseph and Nicodemus have done their work and gone; John has led "to his own" the heart-broken Mother; but others remain, "sitting over against the sepulchre," and looking at the spot "where His body was laid." Again we have little difficulty in recognizing who they represent. There are those whose chief devotion in life is to sit "over against the sepulchre" and to "behold where His body is laid"; hungry souls, whose craving for prayer, and for union with the Lord Whom they have once known, never leaves them, yet who seem to be left very much alone, permitted only to look at the "place where He is laid," and then to go forward and do for Him whatever their love shall suggest, it matters little what. Such souls often have the added agony of not knowing the joy of this abiding.

Summary

1. The honor of the funeral of Our Lord; the layman's place in the Church.

2. The honor of the sepulchre and of the tabernacle.

3. The watchers at the sepulchre represented in all time.

LII.—THE GUARDS

"And the next day which followed the day of the preparation, the chief priests and the Pharisees came together to Pilate, saying: Sir, we have remembered that that seducer said, while He was yet alive: After three days I will rise again. Command, therefore, the sepulchre to be guarded until the third day, lest His disciples come, and steal Him away, and say to the people: He is risen from the dead, so the last error shall be worse than the first. Pilate said to them: You have a guard; go, guard it as you know. And they, departing made the sepulchre sure with guards, sealing the stone."—Matt. xxvii. 62-66.

1. St. Augustine has a famous withering passage of the significance of this last act of "the chief priests and Pharisees." But perhaps he does not dwell as much as might be done on the terrible self-awakening confession that these words imply. They had accepted as evidence against Him His words that He would destroy the Temple. Though the witnesses had not agreed before Annas, yet they had raked the accusation up again when they flung their charges at Pilate. And now, in the most flagrant way, they acknowledge that from the beginning they had understood perfectly what He had meant. Apparently, even the Apostles had not; for St.

John tells us they clearly understood only after the Resurrection. But the chief priests and Pharisees were trained in such language; its interpretation was the study of their lives; and Our Lord spoke to them "in their own tongue" when He made that prophecy. No wonder, then, that all this time it had rankled most in their minds; no wonder, when He was yet alive, it was the source of their chief attack among themselves; and no wonder, now that He was dead, they were compelled to take notice of it.

2. But the folly of contending with Our Lord Jesus Christ! Above all, the folly of setting up our own judgment against the judgment of Our Lord, or of forcing His words to our own sense! These men understood, but they did not believe; or rather it should be said they would not let themselves believe. As on one occasion they had said: "This is a hard saying, and who shall hear it?" confessing that they understood and yet would not believe; as on another occasion they had said: "We have Abraham and the prophets," confessing that they understood and yet would not believe; as many other times they had made the same confession, and yet had chosen to refuse; so now, the habit had been formed, and they found it easy to accept the understanding of the words, yet refused to believe them, and therefore to believe in Him who uttered them.

3. But "God is not mocked." God is not called

an "imposter," a "seducer," with impunity. He rules from end to end mightily; He puts down the mighty from their seat and exalts the lowly; and no one escapes from His rule. Men induce themselves to believe in themselves, where they cannot do so with any show of reason; there must follow the downfall at one time or another, for "the truth is great and will prevail." Something of this must have made that Sabbath-day an anxious one for the chief priests and Pharisees; and the same must have filled the mourners with firm hope, which must have increased with every moment. The sun goes down over the burial of Our Lord with beauty and glory; and the Church has been unable to resist the anticipation of the coming triumph, as she sings her Alleluia the day before.

Summary

1. The self-conviction of the chief priests and Pharisees.
2. The self-delusion of their refusal to believe.
3. The inevitable issue.

CARMELITE MONASTERY